The Great Gatsby
and Modern Times

The Great Gatsby and Modern Times

Ronald Berman

University of Illinois Press
Urbana and Chicago

Publication of this book was made possible in part by a grant
from the University of California at San Diego.

© 1994 by the Board of Trustees of the University of Illinois
Manufactured in the United States of America
C 5 4 3 2 1

This book is printed on acid-free paper.

Library of Congress Cataloging-in-Publication Data

Berman, Ronald.
    The Great Gatsby and modern times / Ronald Berman.
        p.   cm.
    Includes bibliographical references and index.
    ISBN 0-252-02045-6 (cloth : acid-free paper)
    1. Fitzgerald, F. Scott (Francis Scott), 1896–1940. Great Gatsby.
    2. Civilization, Modern—20th century.   I. Title.
    PS3511.I9G824   1994   813'.52—dc20   93-10601
                                                             CIP

For Leonard Garment

Contents

Acknowledgments

I have been greatly helped by the Central University Library of the University of California, San Diego. Needless to say, I have relied on the scholarship of those who have worked on *The Great Gatsby* before me. I owe a debt of gratitude to their effort and insight. James R. Mellow has generously provided important materials on the decade of the twenties, and Milton R. Stern has been the most admirable and judicious of readers. Above all, I am grateful to the dean of Fitzgerald scholars, Matthew J. Bruccoli, for reading the manuscript of this book, providing vigorous critical assistance and opposition, and making it less likely to err.

There is a debt of special gratitude to Barbara and Kathy, my "editors."

Introduction

When Gertrude Stein wrote to F. Scott Fitzgerald in praise of *The Great Gatsby* she drew a certain kind of equivalence: "You are creating the contemporary world much as Thackeray [*sic*] did his in Pendennis and Vanity Fair and this isn't a bad compliment." [Fitzgerald's text is full of recognizable things, but they are related and perceived in special ways. This book attempts to answer the following questions about his creation of that "contemporary world": What does it look like? How is it perceived? What is the nature of time and place? What is its historical moment? What are the economic realities? How do we accumulate ideas about identity? What techniques depict that "contemporary" world? And, finally, are there texts of that world within this text?

It may be best to begin with a genuinely "contemporary" issue. Fitzgerald introduces into his own text a remarkable amount of things manufactured, marketed, advertised, and consumed. They are signs of a new, expansive economy. But they are in many cases also metonymical, reminding us of a new mental landscape. Here is the summation of an argument about the artistic usefulness of cityscape, an argument published two years after *The Great Gatsby* but conducted for at least two decades before it: "Have you ever thought about the sadness that streets, squares, stations, subways, first class hotels, dance halls, movies, dining cars, highways, nature would all exhibit without the innumerable billboards, without show windows . . . without luminous signboards, without the false blandishments of loudspeakers, and imagine the sadness and monotony of meals and wine without polychrome menus and fancy labels." This itemization of the industrial world comes from Cendrars's 1927 piece, "Advertising = Poetry."[2] The visual presence of industrial design had for some time been the subject of serious writing—before the Great War, Ezra Pound, thinking over the geometric repetitions of

1

the lighted windows and skyline of New York had said, "here is our poetry."[3] Pound "establishes a continuity" with another futurist, Marinetti, and Eliot later appropriated the correlatives of industrialism. As Hugh Kenner puts it, Eliot "is undeniably his time's chief poet of the alarm clock, the furnished flat, the ubiquitous telephone, commuting crowds, the electric underground railway."[4] The perception and description of cityscape is part of the literary work of the twenties.

The Great Gatsby devotes much of its narration to the description of industrial things and forms—for example, an apartment loaded with the spoils of production. Its own prose rhythm is interrupted by counterpoint: the beat of engines and the metronomic, empty sound of an unanswered telephone. The story takes place within a geometric grid of streets and avenues. When she first meets Tom Buchanan, Myrtle Wilson is on her way to "a subway train" (31).[5] Chapter 7 is about the life of first-class hotels—and the rest of the text is alive with the mention of places to rent and sell and stay. There are dance halls, rooms that "always . . . throbbed incessantly" (118) with the sound of the blues. There are those big, cool movies around Fiftieth Street, and also the reiterated presence of movie images in magazines; of movie selves imitated by personality. As for billboards, windows, and luminous signs, they overlook much of the novel's action and provide certain meanings.

Fitzgerald is, however, preoccupied with more than the rendition of objective content. The death scenes of Myrtle and Gatsby are problems in the statement of form, not in the statement of affectiveness. In Myrtle's case, a road is intersected by her line of flight. The car moves along a curved line and leaves her kneeling in parabolic form with her left breast "swinging loose like a flap" (107) and her mouth open and "ripped at the corners." Gatsby is last seen moving in circles like those drawn by a compass. Both are studies in stillness and motion. Description is intensely geometrical. It seeks comparison with artifact and mechanism. And if this novel comes from a homemade world, then many parts have been disassembled, strewn through the pages of the text.

The perception of things in the novel reinforces and eventually redefines our perception of relationships. Few other novels insist so continuously on the difficulty of seeing, judging, even of describing what is seen. Although extremely visual, The Great Gatsby is full of barriers to sight and insight. It may be that the dimness of perception of people and things corresponds to the ambiguity of human relationship.

Two of the most important aspects of perception are time and place. But in *The Great Gatsby* their invocation is more than realistic. We are instructed that there are "at least 450 time words in the novel,"[6] yet many of them do the opposite of what we expect. They do not locate us in a chronology of act and experience. Instead, they imply a kind of double vision. It is easy to see that for Gatsby past and present are dangerously undifferentiated—but the reader's sense of time and place is affected also by the way that Nick states his own perceptions and restates the dialogue he remembers. He will do for place what Gatsby does for time: impose upon its specificity the consciousness of what it was—and often what it is not. The text is full of alterations of time and place, reminding us that Eden is on the other side of the Queensboro Bridge, and the abounding blessed isles beyond Long Island Sound.

Fitzgerald's intricate statement of time and place calls our attention to some possible meanings of his text. Throughout the narrative, he alludes to both in interlocking ways. One way is realistic, serving to locate the action in a given chronological sequence over the summer of 1922. We see events, cultural issues, styles, and ideas of this brief period and also of the quarter-century in which it is set. The second kind of time in this novel is connected to an idea of its imbalance like that so recently brought to consciousness by T. S. Eliot in the same year that the novel's events take place. There is a historical world in this text with its own exact chronology, but it subsists within a much deeper temporality.

The historical world is decisively implied, as when the text insists on context. For example, it connects one date, July 5, 1922, with certain events and also with the endless permutations of class and style and self-chosen character in America. The date is just after Independence Day, linked (even being written on the self-expressive form of a timetable) with the progression of names of those who went to Gatsby's. These names suggest social change and personal change and ethnic change; the irresistible forces of social mobility; the alchemy of self-designation; and the "blurring and loss of identity"[7] of American democracy. The combination of dating and naming translates listing into something more complex. The same kind of reasoning ought to be applied to another date established by the text, September 12, 1906. That is the date of Jimmy Gatz's SCHEDULE, with its resolution to study "needed" inventions, that is, those that are conceptually related to a public sense of self; and to read "improving" books or magazines or those that relate the development of the self to models of excellence. The word *improving* has an American history much as the word *earnest* has an English history. One date suggests the dangerously heterogeneous present, the other calls to mind a vanished world of moral certainties and public obligations, the world of Teddy Roosevelt. There are connections throughout Fitzgerald's work between the two worlds.

But in this novel each character has a different sense of time and the text itself differentiates between many ways of locating ourselves in the moving present. We know the timetables for the summer solstice and the commuter train and the escaping years of our lives. Time is connected not only to history but to space. The more Nick Carraway tries to locate himself through the named and known quantities of West Egg on Long Island in North America in the Western Hemisphere the more he finds that he is somewhere he scarcely knows at all. We realize the disparities of time and place when we see the Merton College Library on West Egg; or San Francisco somewhere between Denver and Detroit; or Monte Carlo and Versailles on 158th Street on the West Side. Confusions of time and place impose relativity, affect the coordinates of logic as well as geography. We progress (within a very few pages) from New Haven and Westchester and Louisville and Maine and Georgia and Times Square and Oxford and Paris, Venice and Rome, and the Argonne Forest and "Little Montenegro" to the Pisgah view from the Queensboro Bridge, where all of the above are canceled out in order to see the created world for the first time. Very little is simply descriptive: we are asked to see a sidewalk in Louisville become Jacob's Ladder; and to lift our eyes from the Buchanans' lawn—or from the printed page—is to see something and some place that is not there.

In addition to chronology and sequence, the dating of particulars, and the temporality of being, time in this text means the dating of ideas. Because so much of the information that is released by the text is connected to serial publication, to what its characters read, we are forced to recognize the momentary quality of that information and of the thought it occasionally inspires. Fitzgerald emphasizes the way that ideas already shaped are distorted through dissemination. Ideas are rarely originated in the text. They are communicated and often translated into their dimmest forms. The text identifies the acquisition of ideas, as when Nick recognizes that Gatsby's "biography" is an imitation. He tells Nick about living the life of "a young rajah" (52) in all the capitals of Europe, collecting jewels, hunting big game, and trying to forget a painful love affair of his past. The facts of his life are fictions put together from other fictions. Hugh Kenner writes that even when Gatsby's words are wrong, "the music is right; the cadence of 'painting a little, things for myself only'—cuddling self-deprecation—or of 'trying to forget something very sad that had happened to me long ago.' That is the authentic music, the cello throb of *Collier's* and the *Post,* purveying with slick effrontery the dreams Horatio Alger could never quite realize to himself."[8] Myrtle gets her identity, in part, out of the generically named *Town Tattle* and the scandal magazines of Broadway and moving-picture magazines that redouble the effect of the new medium. They connect entertainment with consumerism, and consumerism with the acquisition of character. Tom gets his ideas from books with long words in them, books that dissipate ideas under the impression that they are radiating them. In this narrative, ideas are bought and paid for. We measure time in many ways, but one of the most interesting is through reliance on "news." Gatsby scans the dailies to find out what has happened to Daisy after her marriage; Nick recognizes Jordan from "a picture" he has seen in the weekly rotogravure; Jordan reads soothingly to Tom from the *Saturday Evening Post.*

Gertrude Stein was interested in "how everybody is doing everything," a phrase that presupposes intense interest in things as disparate as intellectual style and everyday marketing. Miles Orvell covers both meanings in his cultural history of the early twentieth century, invoking the new "visual environment" of industrialism and its fascination for writers. Important elements were "photography, advertisements, and cinema," the modes of commercial image and print that affected and created style. These modes meant more, however, than the sale of commodities. Orvell cites Vachel Lindsay: "American civilization grows more hieroglyphic every day. The cartoons of Darling, the advertisements in the back of the magazines and on the billboards and in the streetcars, the acres of photographs in the Sunday newspapers, make us into a hieroglyphic civilization far nearer to Egypt than to England."[9] One doesn't know about Egypt, but Lindsay does state part of Fitzgerald's repertory. Fitzgerald himself has become a reference point for "how everybody is doing everything." A recent survey of French fashion in the twenties by the Curator of Costume at the Museum of the City of New York begins by invoking his awareness of the new universal style. His statement about Paris—"everything that happened there seemed to have something to do with art"—seems to echo Gertrude Stein. We recall that Jordan Baker's name implies one kind of technology, and we may conclude that her appearance suggests another: "Flattened, impossibly elongated figures attest to Cubist influence as well as that of Marie Laurencin and Modigliani. The asymmetry, geometrically precise pleats and tubular forms of dresses and figures relate directly to painting."[10]

Marketplace relations are the other half of Fitzgerald's observation— and, I think, of Gertrude Stein's. The ultimate product of technique was the self. There were by the early twenties vast numbers of examples of self-construction through commodities, among them Eliot's inventories of cosmetics and lingerie and drying combinations and other instruments of acquired appearance. Edmund Wilson, much closer as an intellectual source to Fitzgerald, had by 1924 issued whole catalogs of observations on the things we bought—among them, for the price of a ticket, the dreams of Broadway.

The marketplace of *The Great Gatsby* is located on Broadway, and the geography of the narrative encircles it, going south on Fifth Avenue to the borders of Murray Hill, then west to Pennsylvania Station, north to those big movies in the fifties, then east again to the Plaza. This area serves not only as the location for Nick's meeting with Wolfshiem, the beginning of his affair with Jordan, and the breakup of Gatsby's own affair with Daisy: Broadway contains the newsstands, movies, and theaters that offer ideas as commodities. The movies are probably most important. Movies sell not only styles but identities; and their effect is redoubled by the magazines and rotogravures and dailies that are the matrix of allusion in the text.

The language of the marketplace infiltrates everywhere. Wilson can't tell the difference between God and an advertisement; Nick sees Jordan for the last time, "thinking she looked like a good illustration" (138). The tactic of placing the description so firmly in marketplace terms states silently the nature of relationship. Feelings and perceptions may even be provided by the marketplace. Marketplace relations dominate relations in the text. Myrtle buys her dog and Tom buys Myrtle. Nick rents, Gatsby buys, the Buchanans inherit. McKee, the idiot photographer who represents so much of the salesmanship in the narrative, lives to peddle his work on the North Shore. One moment in the text reverses the Jamesian theme of Americans abroad: "I was immediately struck by the number of young Englishmen dotted about; all well dressed, all looking a little hungry, and all talking in low, earnest voices to solid and prosperous Americans. I was sure that they were selling something: bonds or insurance or automobiles" (35). Commodities are definitions: Wilson knows that Tom's car is the equivalent of his own going west to start a new life; Gatsby knows that his gorgeous and melodic car establishes his status.

Especially when Myrtle Wilson is involved in the action, we can see what Fitzgerald has learned about the American marketplace. When Myrtle assembles herself, complete to dress, dog, apartment, and dialogue ("My Dear"), we see not only her own vast energies but those of the economy and the new consumer culture. Through Myrtle we become aware of the realm of imitation, hence of the human dynamics of the story. The party at Myrtle's apartment is one of the great messes in literature. Yet everywhere among the fallen are contravening images: "to move about was to stumble continually over scenes of ladies swinging in the gardens of Versailles" (25). These scenes of the aristocracy of Fragonard, Boucher, Watteau, and Le Brun belong now to manufactured interior decoration. They have been stamped out in their thousands. The subject may be French, but the technique is Hogarthian: the apartment is itself an economy, full of objects and commodities that have been duplicated. As his biographer says of Hogarth, "the real, feigned (acted), carved, and painted are all related within a single picture. The richness of literary content cannot be dissociated from the effect of the purely formal elements."[11] In this case there are "scenes" within the scene that both parody and describe. The assembly-line tapestries state high life as Myrtle imagines it, fully clothed, richly at leisure, always dressed for a part. And they remind us, as objects and commodities and replications do throughout the text, that ideas are things.

The characters of *The Great Gatsby* see ideal forms of themselves in film and in magazines. They are conscious, sometimes deeply and emotionally so, of advertisements. The narrative uses a highly intentional language of replication: "picture," "illustration," "advertisement," "photograph," "newspaper reports," "copy," and other things which continually argue that they are as "true" as Gatsby's photograph of Trinity Quad, and as "real" as his father's photograph of the great house on West Egg. But this language prepares us to understand also that how we do everything is theatrical. There is hardly a character in the novel who does not have an ideal self in mind, a self which is constructed or achieved. But the sense of self—even dreams of selfhood—in this story are the products of ideology or market enterprise. The idea of self is often specifically related to magazines and movies. People play at roles and sometimes even seem to have scripts in mind: there is Myrtle, who shows us in her apartment the way she looks after she has become what she thinks she is. We see Tom self-consciously wrapped in the robes of Native Americanism, ready, according to Nick Carraway, to pose for a painting of Civilization on the Barricades. There is Daisy playing always to an audience and, in one startling moment that links the rhetoric of film to text, viewed in front of the gorgeous, empty actress who is her simulacrum. But theatricality is not only a way of expressing desires but of concealing them. We are accustomed to think of *The Great Gatsby* as a story of mobility and change, but it is also a story of disguise, that is to say, of appearing to change while remaining the same.

One of the most powerful oppositions in the book is that between Broadway and Hollywood. Both stand for artifice, but the former stands also for emotional authenticity. Gatsby may be "a regular Belasco" (38) or producer of his own life's theater, but the "act" he puts on is considerably preferable to other kinds of acting and enactment. Daisy is drawn to the distancing, aesthetic and moral, of Hollywood—her genre, so to speak, is film, or at least film romance. Gatsby is a figure of Broadway, a place and an idea with an overwhelming presence in the text. Broadway sells dreams—and even ideologies—but it expresses real desires, calls on real feelings. It is where Gatsby comes back to life as Wolfshiem lifts him out of the street. It is where his guests come from in their "simplicity of heart" (34) that corresponds to his own combination of vulgarity and emotional authenticity. It is Gatsby's milieu, and it becomes Nick's. Very little is emotionally or sexually disguised on Broadway.

Fitzgerald's feeling for the movie houses and poolrooms and restaurants and revues of midtown—he called it a "passion for Broadway"[12]—corresponds to Edmund Wilson's. We see a self-conscious, explicit association between the two writers on this subject. According to Wilson, in 1923, the *Follies* "has in it something of Riverside Drive, of the Plaza, of Scott Fitzgerald's novels."[13] There is, he says, "something wonderful about the *Follies*," and he is taken especially with its "vitality." Like Nick Carraway, Wilson finds himself "haunted" by the brassy, obscene music of city nights.[14] Wilson discriminates, as Fitzgerald does, between the intensely rhythmic flow of music and the "harsh and complicated harmonies" of "nervous intensity"[15] that the city betrays. Both writers associate dissonance with Broadway, and with the revelation of authenticity. But at Gatsby's second party Nick feels "many-colored, many-keyed commotion . . . a pervading harshness" that Daisy plainly does not want to understand.

In terms of technique, we will often see things, landscape and human objects, through the momentary glimpse of film and lens. The text will direct our attention to certain "scenes" by looking at them through the "flicker" of film movement—on Broadway, or crossing the Queensboro Bridge we see a mechanical world through mechanical means. When we look at Tom Buchanan, on our first assessment of him, he becomes for the moment a kind of machine in himself, and our perception of his bodily structure is in fact the perception by a moving-picture lens of an object in front of it. Nothing could be more appropriate than the inspection of one machine, calculated in terms of its force and leverage, by another.

The text is permeated with references to still photography; film development, prints, copies, illustrations, etc. But some of its longest scenes depend on the audience's familiarity with "moving-picture" technique and technology. Possibly the most noticeable thing about such scenes is their silence. Part of Fitzgerald's experiment in this novel is the rendition of gesture that takes the place of speech. There is what seems to be intentional correspondence to the perception of the silent lens. There are certain silent scenes in *The Great Gatsby* that are, I think, openly cinematic, as in the theater view that we get of Tom and Daisy through the pantry window in which they are on stage in the light and we see them from the dark. Such scenes can be reminiscent of film staging, with special kinds of lighting and even props. Or they can suggest the perspective (and even the operation) of lenses. They will at times invoke the idiom of photography, as when expressions on Myrtle's face appear as if they were "objects" in "a slowly developing picture." In addition to film technique there is film allusion. At certain moments in the narrative we are intended to see Daisy and Myrtle through the new mythology (and vocabulary) of social character: Daisy loves to act out the script of the Poor Little Rich Girl while Myrtle echoes many of the social-climbing themes of movies about "working girls" who marry rich and Rise to the Top.

Fitzgerald has a particular strategy for the examination of the meaning of change. He rarely refers himself to history. He had great difficulty, as the novel was composed, in dealing with Gatsby's biography. He clearly has little interest in politics—this is a novel in which parties and Congress and the great issues of the moment are invisible, except through Tom Buchanan's dim refraction of the politics of race and immigration. The novel's extraordinary grasp of change both personal and social is displayed through a different kind of allusion. The issue of change takes part of its definition from texts. Gatsby gets his ideas from books—perhaps because that is how Fitzgerald got his own ideas. Throughout *The Great Gatsby* the passage of time (and the currency or obsolescence of ideas) is marked by texts.

Certain texts themselves enter the text, as in Fitzgerald's retelling of the Horatio Alger plot. Alger is usually perceived as having provided for Fitzgerald and other writers the essential plot of rising from poverty through success in business. But a good deal more seems to have been involved. The Alger stories are full of the kind of resentment about class, style, and wealth that Fitzgerald often expressed in his writing and in the fictions he invented of his own life. Alger applies to Fitzgerald's art and life not only because he tells the great modern story of "rising" to "success" but also because he has such a clear sense of the enemies of promise. Alger is both a guide to the action and a standard of irony.

I have tried to deal also with what Fitzgerald (in "Bernice Bobs Her Hair") called textual "models" of identity. These "models" come from ordained childhood reading. They are identified with the past, not only the idealized perception of childhood itself but the infinitely innocent first decades of the new century in which Fitzgerald grew up. Both before and after *The Great Gatsby* Fitzgerald defined the past in terms of its fiction. But, what one learns in the beginning is as distant from the meaningful supervision of later life as those books in Gatsby's library.

The characters of *The Great Gatsby* absorb ideas and feelings from what is communicated to them. It might be said that their closest relationships are not with each other—and certainly not with family or community or tradition—but with published, advertised, and perceived images and print. As the narrative begins Nick Carraway tells us how far we are from family, tradition, and clan; on the last page of most editions he states our irretrievable distance from historical beginnings. Much of the narrative in between registers the advent of ideas and values from other kinds of sources.

Notes

1. From a letter of May 22, 1925, in Matthew J. Bruccoli and Margaret M. Duggan, eds., *Correspondence of F. Scott Fitzgerald* (New York: Random House, 1980), p. 164.

2. Marjorie Perloff, *The Futurist Moment* (Chicago: University of Chicago Press, 1986), p. 9.

3. Perloff, *The Futurist Moment,* p. 179.

4. Hugh Kenner, *The Mechanic Muse* (New York: Oxford University Press, 1987), p. 25.

5. All citations of the text are from *The Great Gatsby,* ed. Matthew J. Bruccoli (Cambridge: Cambridge University Press, 1991). Page numbers following citations are keyed to this edition.

6. Matthew J. Bruccoli, ed., *New Essays on The Great Gatsby* (New York: Cambridge University Press, 1985), p. 11. And, "exclusive of character names, the second most frequent noun is *time,* with 87 occurrences. (*House* appears 95 times.) *Moment* or *moments* occur 73 times; *day* or *days,* 70; *minute* or *minutes,*

49; *hour* or *hours,* 47; *o'clock,* 26; *year,* 19; *past,* 18. . . . The first striking image in the novel is the Buchanans' lawn "jumping over sun-dials."

7. Robert Emmet Long, *The Achieving of The Great Gatsby* (Lewisburg: Bucknell University Press, 1979), p. 143.

8. Hugh Kenner, *A Homemade World: The American Modernist Writers* (New York: William Morrow, 1975), p. 42. Kenner adds that the events of the narrative of *The Great Gatsby* might have been "ingredients for a *Post* serial."

9. Miles Orvell, *The Real Thing: Imitation and Authenticity in American Culture, 1880–1940* (Chapel Hill: University of North Carolina Press, 1989), pp. 243–44.

10. JoAnne Olian, *Authentic French Fashions of the Twenties* (New York: Dover, 1990), v.

11. Ronald Paulson, *Hogarth: His Life, Art, and Times* (New Haven: Yale University Press, 1974), p. 138.

12. F. Scott Fitzgerald, "My Lost City," in *The Crack-Up,* ed. Edmund Wilson (New York: New Directions, 1945), p. 26.

13. Edmund Wilson, "The Follies as an Institution," in *The American Earthquake* (New York: Farrar Straus Giroux, 1958), p. 51.

14. Wilson, "Bert Savoy and Eddie Cantor of the Follies," in *The American Earthquake,* p. 60.

15. Ibid., p. 59.

1

Contexts

■   In "Echoes of the Jazz Age," written in the early thirties, with a flourish Fitzgerald identified the crucial year of the preceding decade: "May one offer in exhibit the year 1922!"[1] It is the turning-point year in which *The Great Gatsby* takes place. And in the novel he makes it a point to be specific about the dating of his story. In what particular ways does the novel use its moment? Let us look at certain ideas in circulation in the summer of 1922, and in the period around it: ideas that, like that of "civilization," are referential in the text. For Tom Buchanan "civilization" is highly meaningful—and is opposed to his sense of "the modern world." Does he echo a public debate? And, is his anxiety over ideas and social situations possibly derived?

One set of anxieties can probably be discarded. In a 1921 interview Fitzgerald stated that, "except for leaving its touch of destruction here and there, I do not think the war left any real lasting effect. Why, it is almost forgotten right now."[2] Possibly to our surprise there was substantial agreement with this. Leading into the year *The Great Gatsby* takes place, on November 30, 1921, the *New Republic* states of "the new spirit" that worldwide, "improvement is spreading rapidly and is increasing in self-confidence and in positive achievement as well as in volume. It is clearly the expression of a temper radically different from that which prevailed during and after the war." Throughout 1922, the *Saturday Evening Post* showed little interest in a war that had by now receded from the memory of its readers and was no longer good copy. The *Post,* in any case, had many other quarrels to engage in, and there are good reasons for it being a magazine of choice for Tom Buchanan. In 1923, the year of the first publication of *Time,* almost nothing was said in its weekly coverage about war disillusion. The archaeologist of news will find instead that *Time* covers war debts, war finances, and armament limitations without invoking war disillusion. In the early twenties *Time* covered fiction and theater in more detail than it now does, but very little of its critical attention was devoted to books or essays about the lasting, debilitating effect of our experience in the Great War. Much attention, however, was paid by *Time,* other magazines, and by Fitzgerald to certain resentments.

On July 5, 1922, a date to remember, the *New Republic* continued its campaign of national introspection or "interpretation" (the term is from the first sentence of the first issue in 1914) of public events. There was much to interpret, beginning with the industrial war in West Virginia in which coal miners had killed nineteen strike breakers. The editors thought that these unionized miners were identical in class outlook and behavior to those who had recently beaten and tortured black migrant workers in Springfield and East St. Louis. There were troubles enough abroad: the Marines were in Haiti; Ireland was habitually regressive in politics and in culture; and in Germany Walther Rathenau had just been assassinated.[3] But, at least for the *New Republic,* foreign policy was not at this point the main issue: what mattered most in American life was the management of domestic change. There were many anxieties, and traditional kinds of explanation seemed no longer to hold. It seemed, for example, to be no longer useful to think about the relationship of Capital to Labor, or of Democrat to Republican. Politics was a waste of time. In 1922, the public duty was to reassess the aggregate of individual lives that constituted the nation and to bring to bear a new private and public sense of self. Perhaps nothing *could* be done about West Virginia until the values of a "Christian people" were asserted—and recognized. About other things much remained to be done, especially about the dual facts of too much money in circulation, and in too few hands. There was an uneasy sense of the swiftness of social change, and, even more, that it might be unmanageable. The issue of July 5 ended on an especially disquieting note, with a review of recent books on coming of age in America. Its last words were about a new cultural sense of self, about the child no longer "the subject of the parental regent, however wise." In the coming decade, it was plain to see, personal identity would be achieved through "self-direction and self-determination." The author reviewed is Rabbi Stephen S. Wise and his book *Child Versus Parent* is taken for a tract for the times. Undesired social change seems now to begin, literally, at home. Both author and reviewer believe that the growth of social character should indeed be ordered by "self-discipline" but they doubt that will happen. Fitzgerald would write in the early thirties that "the wildest of all generations" was that "which had been adolescent during the confusion of the War."[4] As for self-discipline, that had been stood on its head: the generation of children had "corrupted its elders."

There is one other thing about this issue that is of special interest to novelists: a review of *Ulysses* by Edmund Wilson. Since reading it, "the texture of other novelists seems intolerably loose and careless." *Ulysses* has invalidated traditional kinds of fiction, including, one supposes, books like *This Side of Paradise* and *The Beautiful and Damned*. New fiction will clearly have to be ironic in tone, modernist in technique. Fitzgerald dutifully read *Ulysses* and wrote to Wilson about its personal effect on him.[5] There is more to the effect of modernism on Fitzgerald that needs to be said and I will try to amplify that in later chapters.

Other magazines will of course have other concerns but they too are focused on the overriding theme of change. There is *Vanity Fair,* a publication closer than the *New Republic* to the tactical issues of Fitzgerald's fiction. *Vanity Fair* means also to be interpretative—its motto has, from the first issue in 1913, been "a record of current achievements in all the arts and a mirror of the progress and promise of American life." Its sense of "promise" resonates to Fitzgerald's themes. *Vanity Fair* was (before the advent of the *New Yorker*) the main source for the creation of social identity through high style. It assumed that self-determination operates through consumption. One of its great themes is the acquisition of identity by conscious choice. That choice is exerted through transaction within the marketplace. The primary assumption of the marketplace of style is that we can choose what we want to be without inhibition. A secondary assumption is that diligent consumption, as thoughtful and perhaps as arduous as that of a lifetime of good works, legitimatizes our efforts. When Myrtle Wilson shops at Pennsylvania Station she is by no means being simply materialistic—she displays the care and prudence once associated with the vocation of citizenship. She understands that purchases and styles are meant not to gratify but to display the character of choice—and the choice of character.

Vanity Fair is necessarily about commodities, and its advertisements are as important as any other instructions conveyed by commercial literature. I believe that Fitzgerald took quite seriously the techniques and even the claims of advertising—he did not differentiate it from the rest of "culture" and indeed he used it to enormous advantage in a novel about people whose energies are often bent toward consumption. There are no warnings in *The Great Gatsby* that when we leave love for advertising or for the description of commodities we are moving from a realm of higher to lower seriousness.

Vanity Fair has a powerfully affective sequence of advertisements (nearly all illustrated, with many taking up an expensive full page) of its principal commodities, automobiles. Here they are in order of appearance in the July 1922 issue: the life-changing designs of the Chalmers Six, Oldsmobile, Wills Sainte Claire, Haynes 75, Renault, Winton, Kimball, De lage, Talbot-Duracq, Marmon, D.A.C., Mercedes, Stanley, Elgin, Dusenberg, the three-wheeled Neracar ("a new type of automotive vehicle unlike either an automobile or a motorcycle"), Ford, Le Baron, Rumpler Raindrop, Studebaker, Durant, Stutz, Pierce-Arrow, Cadillac, Sunbeam, Ballot, Packard Twin-Six, Paige, Daniels, Derham, and La Fayette. The August issue will add the Maxwell, Locomobile, Essex, and the Rolls-Royce favored by Gatsby. In relation to all advertisements and text the automobile is by far the most important commodity in the issue. It is as important a symbolic object to *Vanity Fair* as it is to *The Great Gatsby*. Each car has a social character to confer. Some will grant middle-class reliability. Most, however, have more extensive ambitions. The products imply consumers who are themselves "leading," "powerful," and even "perfect." These products confer "esteem," "security," "enjoyment" and, possibly more important, something not likely to be granted often by daily life, complete "satisfaction." In *The Great Gatsby* one of these cars will even turn out to be "triumphant."

Few of the cars on the pages of *Vanity Fair* are less elaborate than Gatsby's, which begins to seem representative rather than extreme. There are not only spare tires but cases for them; there are tools and gauges for mileage, gasoline, and oil; and logs for daily expenses. There are monograms in metal to prove ownership. There are traveling sundials. A special model of the Pierce-Arrow comes equipped with water tank and icebox for cocktail parties; with bottles, glasses, "knives, forks, plates and other picnic paraphernalia." This model also has a Victrola and room for records to play on it. There is a built-in Kodak to memorialize its usage. The Stutz is itself interpretative, "owned and liked by men who have long since passed the Dollar Sign on the road to achievement."

Gatsby seems less idiosyncratic when a magazine of 1922 is opened.

The majority of other commodities in the July issue of *Vanity Fair* are clothes *that* make the man. Advertisements of the 1990s now praise natural impulse and promise individuality within the mass. Ads of the twenties are more socially instructive. They reflect realities, not impulses. We buy underwear because of "The Question of Health." A watch is not an ornament or *jeu d'esprit* but "The Last Essential in Dress." What matters is that which allows us to be "approved" and which turns us into "ladies" and "gentlemen." B.V.D.s suggest neither sexuality nor privacy—they are what a man wears for the last perceivable stage of correctness in the club locker room. It is only natural that a considerable amount of anxiety should be generated because the marketplace is full of those who aspire to mobility but who cannot defend their origins. The marketplace of identity has to avoid the issue tackled by the great novels of social change that kept inner consciousness focused on the past. In the great line of narrative from Dickens to Lawrence and Joyce the problem is not that of achieving status but of reconciling it with one's former, inner—and true—identity. The ads of *Vanity Fair* promise a change of identity so complete that there will be no former self left to argue with.

The Vanity Fair Shopping Service undertakes "to leave the decision" about acquiring a new self through commodities "to Vanity Fair's judgment." It is a judgment much less fallible in its sense of a social self than any individual's is liable to be. There are many ads like this one in magazines of the twenties, providing instructions for those on the margins of class. The marketplace had to formulate character as well as supply demand. Fitzgerald once wrote ad copy himself and was aware of the relationship between style and status: Gatsby leaves the decision about his shirts to a man in England who sends over a "selection" of things each season. Daisy understands not only the plenum of styles but the way they reach Gatsby and what they mean to him.

The ultimate promise about acquired identity is made in *Vanity Fair* by an ad for the La Fayette: "He Who Owns A La Fayette is envied by all who truly love fine things. Quiet, beautiful and strong, this car rules any road it travels." It should be no surprise that after Daisy tells Gatsby indirectly that she loves him, she seeks for her own objective correlative: "You resemble the advertisement of the man. . . . You know the advertisement of the man——" (93). Probably not the man in the

La Fayette ad, but the man whose face is drawn a thousand times a day in the art of commercial realism, a figure perfectly achieved.[6]

But even *Vanity Fair* has second thoughts about "progress and promise." In the May 1922 issue, the omnipresent Hendrik Willem Van Loon had invoked "civilization" in a way that would reverberate throughout the decade.[7] The term will come to mean a great deal to Tom Buchanan in the spring of 1922 and to those he represents. Van Loon writes that after the war, "America has suddenly been called upon to carry forward the work of civilization." We must now provide what an exhausted Old World used to provide, "art and literature and science and music and all the other great accomplishments of the human race." Or, as Tom confusedly puts it in his redaction of profundity, "oh, science and art and all that" (14). By "art" both mean aesthetics in the service of social stasis: realistic images with moral values. But there are some redefinitions also about "the human race." Van Loon adds that civilization as we know it may well vanish, exactly as when "unknown hordes from unknown parts of Asia and Eastern Europe broke through the barriers of Rome and installed themselves amidst the ruins of the old Augustan cities." The modern equivalent of these hordes is "the latest shipment of released Ellis Islanders" who will "make a new home among the neglected residences of your own grandfathers and uncles." The issue was addressed from the other side of the aisle at exactly the same time (May 10, 1922) by the *New Republic,* which concluded that national identity would be changed no matter what people like Van Loon wanted. A "new" kind of "upstart half-breed Americans seem destined to rule the larger American cities for many years in spite of the discomfiture, the dismay and the ineffectual protests of the former ruling class." It is a good description of the political-cultural dialectic—and also of Tom Buchanan and his fears.

Harper's Monthly Magazine in the early twenties had few advertisements and showed little interest in either domestic or national policy. It was very much in the genteel tradition, concerned with manners, the fiction of sensibility, various uses of Nature, the alternatives of city and country life, and the cultural responsibilities of the enlightened middle class. More than one piece in the July 1922 issue sought to be inspirational about America. But the theme so persistent in other texts finds expression here also: we were better off before times changed. The open-

ing essay, "What Happens to Pioneers," is about a country once un-
troubled by mass migrations from Europe to America—or from South
to North. It insists that before the twentieth century, ownership and
working of the land themselves constituted moral character. As for the
settlement of the wilderness—that had been an act of national altruism.
It is bad enough that the change in population from country to city-
based has wrought a change in our national character—much worse is
the effect of ideas about our past. A certain nameless reviewer for the
New Republic (clearly infected by the spirit of Veblen and of Beard) is
the villain of this piece in *Harper's*. That reviewer, obviously a modern
materialist with no regard for the meaning of American history, has converted "The dreaming builders" of our union, who were entirely altruis-
tic, into "real-estate speculators, usurers, merchants, brokers," and petti-
fogging lawyers. The "mystic exaltation" of the Founding Fathers has
been reduced to mere "pecuniary interest." Their motive for developing
the wilderness is now interpreted by moderns as being only the desire
to profit from it. American history, according to such new, deracinated
intellectuals, *is an exact counterpart of contemporary history*. There are two
main sources of resentment in this piece: that the innocent past should
be so distant from the corrupt present; and that it should be judged by
"modern" ideas.

The July *Harper's* ends with the "Editor's Easy Chair" in which the
reader is warned that "A man's most difficult antagonist is within himself, and the same is apt to be true of nations." The specific issue is
American national life perceived in terms ("anxieties," loss of "con-
fidence," and of "balance") that are clearly not political but moral-
psychological. This kind of transference is one of the great modes of
periodical literature and of the entire enterprise of social commentary.
There are some good reasons for the public being addressed as if it were
in a continual state of moral crisis. In an age of limited government there
are necessarily limited expectations. It is rare for the editorialists of the
early twenties to appeal to state or federal agencies. They sermonize instead. And they persist in understanding national issues as if they *were*
moral issues. This is as true of Irving Babbitt as it is of Tom Buchanan.
It is as if national character were perceived as an enlarged form of individual character. Within that tradition the editor of *Harper's* looks back

at the nineteenth century, and says that "the old way" of doing things "has not worked well" for us. The truth may be that twentieth-century problems are not amenable to nineteenth-century solutions. *There is an unbridgeable distance between our history and our selves.*

If we are to judge from this limited sample, public debate on the subject of true Americanism was mournful and confused. As for American "civilization," that debate was even angrier and uglier than Tom Buchanan's. The term "civilization" was everywhere in use for the expression of anxiety. It was often used as a code word meaning innocent American national character before mass immigration and Emancipation—and before the loathsome effects of modernity.

■

During a "polite" and "pleasant" dinner on East Egg Nick Carraway unconsciously engages a national dialectic: it takes no more than saying, "You make me feel uncivilized, Daisy" (13). Nick says that he "meant nothing in particular by this remark, but it was taken up in an unexpected way" (14). From this point on Tom Buchanan is cued to debate "civilization," and the text begins its refraction of ideas from print. As Tom says of his current favorite book, "everybody ought to read it" (14), and the implication is that ideas do in fact circulate from texts. Fitzgerald has gone to some trouble to indicate—in a very pointed communication from Nick to the reader—that an eruption has occurred that reveals underlying truths. Beneath the surface of a "pleasant" evening is resentment, even rage if we are to judge from what seems to be its displaced forms in Tom. We get from "art" and "science" to race very quickly. There is a strange parallel between this passage and another passage published a few years before, in 1919, which also moves volcanically from "art" to "civilization." William Winter's life of David Belasco complacently views the state of Broadway productions and then suddenly precipitates national resentments about the visible evidences for historical change:

> The spirit of our country is and long has been one of pagan Materialism, infecting all branches of thought, and of unscrupulous Commercialism, infecting all branches of action. Foreign ele-

ments, alien to our institutions and ideals as to our language and
our thoughts,—seditious elements, ignorant, boisterous, treach-
erous, and dangerous—have been introduced into our population
in immense quantities, interpenetrating and contaminating it in
many ways: in the face of self-evident peril and of iterated warnings and protests, immigration into the United States has been
permitted during the last twenty years of about 15,000,000 persons—including vast numbers of the most undesirable order. We
call ourselves a civilized nation—but civility is conspicuous in our
country chiefly by its absence. Gentleness is despised. Good manners are practically extinct. Public decorum is almost unknown.
We are notoriously a law-contemning people. The murder rate—
the *unpunished* murder rate—in our country has long been a world
scandal. Mob outrage is an incident of weekly occurrence among
us. Our methods of business, approved and practised, are not only
unscrupulous but predatory. Every public conveyance and place
of resort bears witness to the general uncouthness by innumerable signs enjoining the most elemental decency. . . . The tone of
the public mind is to a woeful extent sordid, selfish, greedy. In our
great cities life is largely a semi-delirious fever of vapid purpose
and paltry strife, and in their public vehicles of transportation the
populace—men, women, and young girls—are herded together
without the remotest observance of common decency,—mauled
and jammed and packed one upon another in a manner which
would not be tolerated in shipment of the helpless steer or the
long-suffering swine.[8]

The suddenness of transference from "art" to "civilization" says something about the way Tom Buchanan's mind works, or fails to work. Winter clearly feels that the movement from one kind of statement about the
art of theater to another kind of statement about the nature of "civilization" is appropriate *and that it makes sense.*

Daisy and Jordan make fun of Tom but they do not seriously challenge his ideas about civilization. In fact, when Daisy reveals her own
ideas she says something of their sources. She has many doubts, and
they come from "the most advanced people" who think that "every-

thing's terrible anyhow" (17). We are faced in the right direction, invited to agree with those who in 1922 argue that life is unsatisfactory. Daisy's sources are cultural pessimists—there is a word for it, *Kulturpessimismus,* or the belief that modernity is without soul or public morality, and that a return to the values of the past is the only possible solution. It was a position for those opposed to the effects of democracy, in America as well as Germany. Pessimism about "civilization" was often expressed in a language strikingly similar to Tom's. In 1920 George Santayana began *Character and Opinion in the United States* with this assertion: "Civilization is perhaps approaching one of those long winters that overtake it from time to time. A flood of barbarism from below may soon level all the fair works of our Christian ancestors, as another flood two thousand years ago levelled those of the ancients."[9]

Related issues were not confined to a lunatic fringe, and they were heavily publicized by magazines and newspapers. In 1923 the celebrated *Study of American Intelligence* by McDougall and Brigham appeared, stating that "the intellectual superiority of our Nordic groups over the Alpine, Mediterranean and negro groups has been demonstrated."[10] The *New York Times* and the American Museum of Natural History agreed. Tom Buchanan would not have been perceived as a crank in the period from 1921 to 1923. He would have compared favorably with some members of Congress. He would have been understood as being under the respectable wing of the amateur anthropologists Madison Grant and Lothrop Stoddard, and of George Horace Lorimer, editor of the *Saturday Evening Post.* A modern historian observes that Grant, a notable racist, "inspired" other writers, and that he was the focus of "sympathetic comments in the editorials of such influential publications as the New York *Times* and the *Saturday Evening Post.*"[11] Grant Overton's *American Nights Entertainment* of 1923 has much to say about national figures whose ideas are assimilated by people like Tom:

> Prophecy is a very old business. It has become our habit to
> think of ourselves as a people without prophets; and yet there was
> never a time when mankind had more seers or more interesting
> ones. What is H. G. Wells but a prophesier, and from whom do we
> receive counsel if not from Mr. Chesterton? Mr. Shaw is our Job's

comforter, and George Horace Lorimer, on the editorial page of Saturday Evening Post, calls us to repentance. A few years ago I had the adventure of reading Madison Grant's *The Passing of the Great Race,* an impassioned proclamation of the merits of the blond Nordic race, and a lamentation over its decay. At that time such a book was in the nature of a revelation whether you gave faith to its assertions and proofs or scoffed at them. The thing that struck me was the impossibility (as it seemed to me) of any reader remaining unmoved; I thought him bound to be carried to a high pitch of enthusiastic affirmation or else roused to fierce resentment and furious denial. And so, in the event, I believe it mainly turned out. At that time, although he was the author of several books, I had not heard of Lothrop Stoddard, unless as a special writer and correspondent for magazines. It was not until April 1920, that *The Rising Tide of Color Against White World-Supremacy* was published. Even so, attention is not readily attracted to a book of this type. Many who have since read it with excitement knew nothing of the volume until, in a speech at Birmingham, Alabama, on 26 October, 1921, President Harding said: "Whoever will take the time to read and ponder Mr. Lothrop Stoddard's book on *The Rising Tide of Color* . . . must realise that our race problem here in the United States is only a phase of a race issue that the whole world confronts."[12]

According to the *Saturday Evening Post,* Stoddard's work attracted "an extraordinary amount of attention" and was recognized as "the first successful attempt to present a scientific explanation of the worldwide epidemic of unrest."[13] He was a household name, which is probably why he is encountered in Tom's household as "this man Goddard" (14) who has written "The Rise of the Coloured Empires."

In 1924 there was much political discourse over American character in Congress, and much argument in print. In a volume at least as well known as Santayana's, Irving Babbitt's *Democracy and Leadership,* the following was stated: "We are assured, indeed, that the highly heterogeneous elements that enter into our population will, like various instruments in an orchestra, merely result in a richer harmony; they will, one may reply, provided that, like an orchestra, they be properly led. Otherwise the outcome may be an unexemplified cacophony. This question of leadership is not primarily biological, but moral." [14] One admires the qualification, but the thrust of argument remains the same: pessimism over those of us who are neither Nordic nor Christian. But Babbitt was infinitely better than most on this issue: in 1925 *Reader's Digest* carried a Madison Grant piece from an earlier issue of the *Forum,* which reads as if it were designed for a Tom Buchanan who had briefly flickered into consciousness over the immigration debate. Grant's essay, "America for the Americans," argues not only against the admission into the United States of black or yellow peoples but also of Germans, inassimilable because of their guttural speech and mannerisms (the war was not adduced). During the early twenties it was widely thought that Germans were insufficiently Nordic. Grant uses the same kind of vocabulary as Tom: "our institutions are Anglo-Saxon and can be maintained by Anglo-Saxons and by other Nordic peoples in sympathy with our culture." [15]

To return to the year of the novel's events: here are two passages that may indicate what we now call intertextuality. The first is from John Higham's history of immigration. It is about a series of articles that Kenneth Roberts wrote for the *Saturday Evening Post* in 1920 and that appeared in book form under the title *Why Europe Leaves Home* in 1922. Roberts cast his findings into the framework of the Nordic theory, concluding that a continuing flood of Alpine, Mediterranean, and Semitic immigrants would inevitably produce "a hybrid race of people as worthless and futile as the good-for-nothing mongrels of Central America and Southeastern Europe." [16] The second passage, from *The Great Gatsby,* seems to be a mere interlude: "Inside, the crimson room bloomed with light. Tom and Miss Baker sat at either end of the long couch and she read aloud to him from the 'Saturday Evening Post'—the words, murmurous and uninflected, running together in a soothing tune. The lamplight, bright on his boots and dull on the autumn-leaf yellow of her hair, glinted along the paper as she turned a page with a flutter of slender muscles in her arms" (17–18).

There is action and meaning at this moment, although it would seem to be a pause in the narrative. Fitzgerald's text reminds us of the existence of other texts. The enormous, imitative enterprise of mass literacy is perceptibly within the consciousness of characters in his own text. What Tom is hearing we will never know, but we can expect that the ideas of the moment are being read to him, and that they too are soothing and uninflected. More is involved than Norman Rockwell covers.

■

The relationship between race and religion and culture had its critics, among them Harold Stearns, who argued against it in *Civilization in the United States* (1922). According to Stearns, "whatever else American civilization is, it is not Anglo-Saxon . . . we shall never achieve any genuine nationalistic self-consciousness as long as we allow certain financial and social minorities to persuade us that we are still an English colony."[17] But it was, by 1922, too late to sort out distinctions—the political debate over immigration from eastern and southern Europe made them easy to cloud over. Even *Civilization in the United States* had to acknowledge the current theory and its vocabulary. Other contributions, for example Geroid Robinson's essay on race, admit that "the attitude of both Northerners and Southerners is somewhat coloured by the fear that the blacks will eventually overrun the country."[18] The essay of Louis Reid on small towns celebrates the "true American civilization," that is, national life before the arrival of Catholics and Jews.[19] Walter Pach, who was reasonably enlightened and has been praised as an art critic by E. H. Gombrich, found himself dependent on race and religion as determinants, arguing for an "art-instinct accumulated in a race for centuries." In the case of literature, he said that instinct belonged to "the Anglo-Saxon race."[20] Stating this was the only way he could conceive of the inherent ability of Americans to produce the cultural proofs of their existence.

The March 1, 1922, issue of the *New Republic* carried the introductory chapter of Walter Lippmann's forthcoming *Public Opinion,* and in this chapter he warned the audience "that under certain conditions men respond as powerfully to fictions as they do to realities." Fictions might be true (or false) scientific theories; they might even be "complete hallucinations"—but they were representations of the environment that determined our responses to it. Some fictions might be beneficial—useful without being accurate—but those abroad in 1922 were apt to be neither. In *Public Opinion,* Lippmann describes fictions corresponding to—identical to—the theories that Tom Buchanan raises in the first and seventh chapters of *The Great Gatsby.* [21] Lippmann's list of current fictions in "news" (he took special pains to distinguish "news" from "truth") are Tom's bugbears: ancestry and American history; race and nationality; and in particular the ideology of "Anglo-Saxons." At the heart of the Lippmann thesis is the premise that these issues, important though they may be in themselves, have become demonized by their public discussion. In both Lippmann and Fitzgerald the conveyance of ideas by print results in an intellectual tragicomedy. It is useful to see Lippmann's reaction to what Fitzgerald was to call "stale" ideas: "The more untrained a mind, the more readily it works out a theory that two things which catch its attention at the same time are causally connected. . . . In hating one thing violently, we readily associate with it as cause or effect most of the other things we hate or fear violently. They may have no more connection than smallpox and alehouses, or Relativity and Bolshevism, but they are bound together in the same emotion. . . . it all culminates in the fabrication of a system of all evil, and of another which is the system of all good. Then our love of the absolute shows itself." [22] It is wise, thought-provoking, and related to one of Fitzgerald's problems in the writing of *The Great Gatsby.* Fitzgerald was no political scientist but he did need to describe the effect of political ideas upon personality and the manifestations of personality. We infer not that Tom Buchanan is either a Democrat or Republican but that within him there really is a "love of the absolute" that wants to "show itself." In essence, psychological necessity chooses belief.

H. L. Mencken agreed to a certain extent. His was eventually the most crushing rebuttal to the fiction of Anglo-Saxon civilization. Mencken's essay on the failure of Anglo-Saxon civilization (1923) was reprinted in *Prejudices: Fourth Series* (1924). But as early as 1917, in an essay on Howells, Mencken had identified what others thought was the *problem* of American democracy as its *nature:* our system worked not despite but because of "the essential conflict of forces among us." [23] In this respect Mencken was more political than either Santayana or Babbitt—and very much more political than either Pound or Eliot. The point of the 1923 essay was not only that the country needed new immigrants but that (and his essay takes on the form of a narrative) the old ones, who now called themselves natives, had failed dismally to establish any kind of "civilization" of their own. Mencken writes about the proud, vainglorious and ignorant culture-hero, or would-be culture-hero, the anxiety-ridden Anglo-Saxon whose "defeat is so palpable that it has filled him with vast alarms, and reduced him to seeking succor in grotesque and extravagant devices. In the fine arts, in the sciences and even in the more complex sorts of business the children of the later immigrants are running away from the descendants of the early settlers. . . . Of the Americans who have come into notice during the past fifty years as poets, as novelists, as critics, as painters, as sculptors and in the minor arts, less than half bear Anglo-Saxon names. . . . So in the sciences."[24] Mencken's Anglo-Saxon is constitutionally a bully, hence his many acts of aggression against social change are accompanied by "desperate efforts" of "denial and concealment." The Anglo-Saxon's "political ideas are crude and shallow. He is almost wholly devoid of esthetic feeling. The most elementary facts about the visible universe alarm him, and incite him to put them down. Educate him, make a professor of him, teach him how to express his soul, and he still remains palpably third-rate. He fears ideas almost more cravenly than he fears men. His blood, I believe, is running thin; perhaps it was not much to boast of at the start."

As Harry E. Barnes observed in the *American Mercury* in 1924, the issue was very much one of "ideas" and public opinion: Madison Grant's work on the superiority of Nordic "civilization" was itself "a literary re-hash of Gobineau and Houston Stewart Chamberlain." And even Grant was "progressively debased" as his book became "widely disseminated," and decanted into Lothrop Stoddard.[25] By the time such ideas reach Tom Buchanan they exist in the form in which he states them.

■

The Anglo-Saxon fears the loss of his "civilization" and that fear is easily confused with conscience. He continually justifies what he does by the illusion of keeping faith with history. Mencken has created a character in a historical drama who responds to the issues of the moment and reminds us of the issues in Fitzgerald's text. Tom seems not only to have read many texts but to originate in them. He is obsessed with acquired ideas. So much so that he expresses a great many of them in the quarrel at the Plaza at a moment when we expect other passions of body and mind. Tom is faced with his wife's lover, with the idea of love itself, but the argument over Daisy takes the form of a lecture on *Kulturbolchewismus*. Tom orates about house, home, and family; about nobodies from nowhere; and about the various abominations of "the modern world" (101). His ideas have traveled a long way from Irving Babbitt and Santayana, from Grant and Stoddard to their reification by mass media. He is so confused by ideas transmitted from mind to media that he can perceive Gatsby only as an epiphenomenon of "the modern world."[26] As for Daisy, to her embarrassment she realizes that Tom sees her only as part of the "institutions" he defends.

As if following a script written by H. L. Mencken, Tom discourses in the first chapter about the arts and sciences and "civilization" itself. He later comes to view Gatsby as a kind of problem in modern institutions. Tom is, like Mencken's satirized Anglo-Saxon, enormously alarmed by the "elementary facts about the visible universe": "pretty soon the earth's going to fall into the sun—or wait a minute—it's just the opposite—the sun's getting colder every year" (92). Fitzgerald has added to Mencken's text a kind of strategic entropy of both world and mind imagining it. When Tom begins his lecture on civilization in the first chapter the reader is tempted to write him off as a crank, which is probably the wrong thing to do. It seems logical because Tom cannot convince anyone with an independent mind of his views on history or national destiny. But there are no independent minds in his household. Daisy and Jordan do not openly disagree—in fact, they go along. They find him ridiculous but acceptable. As Jordan later says, settling differences at the Plaza, "We're all white here" (101). It would appear, by the simplest kind of extension, that there are few independent minds anywhere else.

Tom agonizes over adultery and divorce. He is alarmed into reflection over race and class. He is irrational about all those who would "throw everything overboard and have intermarriage between black and white" (101). Even a moralist must have exceptional capacities for outrage to worry about all these things. Unless, of course, his whole concept of identity were involved.[27] Part of that identity has been provided by association: the text introduces him as "Tom Buchanan of Chicago," which does more than mimic society-page seriousness. He is part of a place, and his opinions are approximations of Chicago opinions. His home-town (he and Daisy try "to settle down" (61) there after their marriage) was the most racially troubled and intolerant city in the North. Indus-try in the early twenties encouraged a migration of black workers from Georgia and Alabama to the factories of the Midwest. It was a cause of great concern because it raised the price of labor in the South. And, of course, the migrants ran up against a new phenomenon in Ameri-can life, persecution from the side that won the Civil War. In so doing, they caused a tremendous revaluation in national life. The notorious Chicago riots were caused by confrontations over jobs, housing, and beachfront recreation. The consequence was the formation of national opinion largely in favor of racism. We recall that Tom worries in the first chapter of *The Great Gatsby* about the white race being "dominant" and keeping "control" of its civilization (both here and abroad). He was not much different from, say, the *New York Times* of July 23, 1919: "The majority of Negroes in Washington before the great war, were well-behaved . . . most of them admitted the superiority of the white race and troubles between the two races were unheard of."[28]

When Tom articulates his ideas we can see some of their likely sources and understand the allusions. But Fitzgerald's text is not a tract; it is concerned with motive as well as ideology. Idea is related to act. We recall Tom's grabbing Nick's arm, bruising Daisy, and breaking Myrtle's nose, as well as his general foaming at the mouth on the subject of marriage. Tom is three-dimensional and is equipped with a number of anxieties connected to his ideas, or to his need for ideas. For ex-ample, he seems fixated upon "I" and "we." He fears "all kinds" (81), in itself a phrase of psychological interest. He talks about "people" (who are unidentified) "sneering" at things sacred to him (101). This too seems meaningful, because the matter has been turned into psycho-drama. Max Scheler's classic study of *Ressentiment,* written in the decade before *The Great Gatsby,* suggests that Fitzgerald understood the con-nection of idea to personality. Scheler depicts the internal language of resentment, which says to itself, "I can forgive everything, but not that you *are*—that you are *what* you are—that I am not what you are."[29] There is no textual connection, but there is a clear parallel between this mode of thought and Tom's litany about Nordic selves: "I am and you are and you are and—" (14). Tom speaks a language of absolute subjectivity. He has invested his needs in ideas, which is to say in allowable aggressions. If he is in fact a representative figure then he says much for Fitzgerald's view of the cultural moment.

We enter the narrative of *The Great Gatsby* to the description of universe, earth, hemisphere, and ocean. Throughout the story the skies will turn, with their silent commentary on the meanings we define as history. In the summer of 1922 we have been separated from the past. Given the anemic description of his family, Nick conveys that his own past has not much to recall. We gather that from the limit on his articulation of its values. He has been given the least useful of social virtues, a kind of passive toleration. It is as if all the moral energy of the nineteenth century had dwindled into good manners.

The novel begins with mention of two important events in national consciousness, the Civil War and the Great War of 1914–18. Neither holds Nick's attention for more than a moment. Hemingway was to make a career out of recollections of his war; Fitzgerald understands things differently. For him the war is a checkpoint in history, a barrier to the influence of the past. His imagination is sociological. Nick dreams neither of the past nor of the war but rather of the new agenda of the twenties—banking and credit and investment.

The postwar world is free of the past and of its institutions, but it is not free of its own false ideas. When Tom Buchanan informs Nick and the reader that "Civilization's going to pieces" (14), he has probably never said truer words. But he is of course displaying more than he describes. He echoes a vast national debate about immigration, race, science, and art. There is something seriously wrong in America—yet it may be Tom's own class and type that is responsible. He represents a group as idle and mindless as that excoriated by Carlyle in *Past and Present.* There is something wrong with the immoral pursuit of wealth by historical figures like James J. Hill—except that inherited possession seems no better. Fitzgerald's rich boys often pose as guardians of tradition and often adduce a false relationship to public values.

The more we hear about "civilization" in the text and the more we experience its style and morality the more we, like Nick Carraway, make our own withdrawal from the historical moment. History in *The Great Gatsby* can rarely be taken at face value—perhaps it is as suspect as biography. When Tom alludes to his favorite racial or geographical or class prejudices (and when Daisy plays to them) a public dialogue is refracted. The most interesting thing about that dialogue is that many of those "advanced" people who deplore civilization in America *are considerably less attractive than Tom Buchanan.* He only echoes their discourse. What matters is not the specific character (if there is any) to his ideas about "science" or "art" but his reflection of a historical moment in which their discussion is more poisonous than his own. In the summer of 1922 there will be very little use in his appealing to profound texts or Daisy appealing to the most advanced people or Nick appealing to the values of the past—or the reader appealing to a larger and more confidence-inspiring set of standards beyond those governing the action. The allusive context of the novel is meant to disturb and disorient. It is as if Fitzgerald had Balzac in mind, and, describing a milieu in which all things are permitted, made it impossible for protagonists or readers to bring to bear morals and other norms.

As for the issue of "Civilization," that was not to be adjudicated by the defenders (and inventors) of the American past. In 1924, while Fitzgerald was thinking over the story that would become *The Great Gatsby,* the *American Mercury* (April 1924) had published a sardonic study of character acquired through consumption: It was richly attentive to certain kinds of ads that showed consumers "how to rise quickly" and "how to become" something other than they were.[30] It noted the increased use of phrases like "wonderful," "astounding," "amazing" and "miraculously" applied to personal change and betterment. In the marketplace of ideas personal identity was itself to become a commodity.

Notes

1. F. Scott Fitzgerald, "Echoes of the Jazz Age," in *The Crack-Up,* ed. Edmund Wilson (New York: New Directions, 1945), p. 15.

2. Frederick James Smith, "Fitzgerald, Flappers and Fame," in *The Romantic Egoists,* ed. Matthew J. Bruccoli, Scottie Fitzgerald Smith, and Joan P. Kerr (New York: Charles Scribner's Sons, 1974), p. 79.

3. The editors feared as a consequence the domination of western Europe by a "militaristic France." Peter Gay writes in *Weimar Culture* (New York: Harper & Row, 1970) that the murder of Walther Rathenau was part of the celebration of the youth culture of the twenties. According to one of Rathenau's assassins, Ernest-Walter Techow, "The younger generation" was "striving for something new, hardly dreamed of. They smelled the morning air. They gathered in themselves an energy charged with the myth of the Prussian-German past, the pressure of the present and the expectation of an unknown future" (p. 87).

4. Fitzgerald, "Echoes of the Jazz Age," p. 15.

5. In a letter to Edmund Wilson the week before the review appeared Fitzgerald admitted that Joyce had caused him to think of his own family history: "I have *Ullyses* [sic] from the Brick Row Bookshop & am starting it. I wish it was layed in America—there is something about middle-class Ireland that depresses me inordinately—I mean gives me a sort of hollow, cheerless pain. Half of my ancestors came from just such an Irish strata or perhaps a lower one. The book makes me feel appallingly naked" (*The Crack-Up,* p. 260). To use the terminology of James R. Mellow, an "invented" life might naturally proceed from these feelings, and a heightened perception of assumed identity in others.

6. "The Unspeakable Egg," a Fitzgerald story that appeared in the *Saturday Evening Post* (July 12, 1924) has the line, "he reminded her of an advertisement for a new car." Reprinted in Matthew J. Bruccoli, ed., *The Price Was High: The Last Uncollected Stories of F. Scott Fitzgerald* (New York: Harcourt Brace Jovanovich, 1979), 128.

7. For a sense of Van Loon's standing see the immensely favorable review of *The Story of Mankind* by Charles A. Beard in the December 21, 1921, issue of *The New Republic*. See also the full-page ad for Van Loon's book, with many blurbs, in the February 1, 1922, issue.

8. William Winter, *The Life of David Belasco,* 2 vols. (New York: Moffat, Yard and Company, 1918) 2:424–27. If there is a solution to Winter's problem that lies in converting art to the display of domestic virtue and history to anti-modernism:

> If true civilization is to develop and live in our country, such conditions, such a spirit, such ideals, manners, and customs as are widely prevalent among us to-day, must utterly pass and cease. The one rational hope that they will so disappear lies in disseminating EDUCATION. . . . For that education Society must look largely to the ministry of the arts and, in particular, to the rightly conducted Theatre. . . . Few managers have been able to take or to understand that view of the Stage. David Belasco was one of them. It is because his administration of his "great office" has been, in the main, conducted in the spirit of a zealous public servant; because for many years he maintained as a public resort a

beautiful theatre, diffusive of the atmosphere of a pleasant, well-ordered home, placing before the public many fine plays, superbly acted, and set upon the stage in a perfection of environment never surpassed anywhere and equalled only by a few of an earlier race of managers, of which he was the last, that David Belasco has, directly and indirectly, exerted an immense influence for good and is entitled to appreciative recognition, enduring celebration, and ever grateful remembrance.

9. George Santayana, *Character and Opinion in the United States* (New York: Doubleday, 1956), vi.

10. Cited by Geoffrey Perrett, *America in the Twenties,* (New York: Simon & Schuster, 1982), p. 79.

11. John Higham, *Strangers in the Land,* (New York: Atheneum, 1965), p. 271.

12. Grant Overton, *American Nights Entertainment* (New York: D. Appleton Company, George Doran Company, Doubleday, Page & Co., Charles Scribner's Sons, 1923), pp. 380–81. I am grateful to James R. Mellow for pointing this book out to me and copying out the passage cited.

13. Overton, *American Nights Entertainment,* pp. 382–83.

14. Irving Babbitt, *Democracy and Leadership* (Boston: Houghton Mifflin, 1924), p. 245. Henry Adams, Henry James, Santayana, Babbitt, Eliot, and Pound are like the *Kulturpessimisten* of Weimar. See the account of the battle against modernity in Walter Lacquer's *Weimar* (New York: Perigee, 1974), pp. 78f. For this side of the Atlantic there is good recent coverage in Eric Sigg's *The American T. S. Eliot* (Cambridge: Cambridge University Press, 1989), pp. 110f. Here is Sigg's account of Henry James on civilization versus immigration: "For James, ethnic pluralism jeopardized social order and cultural achievement. He assumed that America should and could produce art equal to that of Europe. He further assumed that American high culture would arise from distinctively American elements in the country's tradition, from shared assumptions about education, morality, and manners, and most important, from a common language used and preserved self-consciously. Immigrants offer James another instance of an American incongruity that is at least bathetic indecorum and at worst surrealist horror" (p. 129).

See also Samuel G. Blythe's lead article "Flux," *Saturday Evening Post,* August 19, 1922, pp. 3f. On political leadership Blythe says that "Politics in this country is now guerrilla warfare. It is not even that. It may best be compared to operations by bodies of indignant and disgusted citizens, in various parts of the country, without communication or ordered plan, getting together from sense of protest and going out and shooting in the dark, hoping they may hit something: but shooting anyhow. There is nothing coherent about our politics. There is nothing much articulate about it in its present state. The prime motive in all our demonstrations is protest. The actuating spirit is change." All things are relative: Blythe has a ferocious attack on "the increasing interference of government in private affairs." Liberals distrusted government performance; conservatives like Blythe distrusted its powers, further reasons for the constant adjuration to Americans to be more moral and more Christian.

15. Madison Grant, "America for the Americans," *Reader's Digest* (October 1925) 367–68.

16. Higham, *Strangers in the Land,* p. 273.

17. Harold E. Stearns, ed., *Civilization in the United States* (London: Jonathan Cape, 1922), vii.

18. Ibid., p. 355.

19. Ibid., p. 295.

20. Ibid., p. 228.

21. Walter Lippmann, *Public Opinion* (New York: Macmillan, 1922), pp. 317–65.

22. Ibid., pp. 154–56. See the powerful piece by Augustus Thomas, "The Print of My Remembrance, *Saturday Evening Post,* July 8, 1922, pp. 24f. Thomas apologizes for writing in a good part for a charitable Jewish physician in *As A Man Thinks,* a one-act play at the Lambs, "instead of having him ridiculed as he generally was in the theater." Thomas attributes racial hatred to the Jewish willingness to work as perceived by the more neglectful and lazy "Anglo-Saxon temperament" (94). Even between liberals and conservatives—racism aside—the debate on cultural differences was framed in terms of the distinction between "Anglo-Saxon" and the rest.

23. H. L. Mencken, *A Mencken Chrestomathy* (New York: Vintage, 1982), p. 491.

24. Ibid., pp. 171–77.

25. See "The Drool Method in History," *American Mercury,* January 1924, pp. 31f.

26. See Perrett, *America in the Twenties,* pp. 159–60: "In 1890 there had been one divorce for every seventeen marriages; by the late twenties there was one for every six. . . . novels, plays, and works of social criticism steadily derided marriage as an outmoded institution, something the modern world could well do without. There were confident predictions that marriage would die out before the end of the century."

27. I disagree with the view that American history is present in the text only to the extent that the "materialism" of "the modern American upper class" betrays our national origins. (See Kermit W. Moyer, "*The Great Gatsby:* Fitzgerald's Meditation on American History," in *Critical Essays on F. Scott Fitzgerald's The Great Gatsby,* ed. Scott Donaldson (Boston: G.K. Hall, 1984), pp. 215f. Tom is said to have a "materialist orientation" and "Daisy represents the materialism of her class." But Tom and Daisy are rarely seen evaluating things

according to cost nor do they judge experience by material standards. Tom's mind is directed by texts and ideas that, far from having anything to do with materialism, are perfervid distortions of idealism.

28. Cited by Perrett in *America in the Twenties,* p. 88.

29. Max Scheler, *Ressentiment* (Glencoe: Free Press, 1961), p. 52. *Das Ressentment* appeared in 1915.

30. "American Boobology: A Survey of Current National Advertising Campaigns," *American Mercury,* April 1924, pp. 457–58.

2

Time and Place

■   When Fitzgerald reconsidered his early success he was struck by the indeterminacy of his experience in New York: "Within a few months after our embarkation on the Metropolitan venture we scarcely knew any more who we were and we hadn't a notion what we were."[1] To judge from the text of *The Great Gatsby,* "where" may be as much a matter of doubt as "who" or "what."

Setting and moment in *The Great Gatsby* seem realistic; enough so for the novel to be constantly adduced by social historians. But there is more than one kind of time in the narrative, and more than one kind of place. There is necessarily more than one kind of literary strategy at work. In July 1925 Shane Leslie wrote to Fitzgerald in praise of *The Great Gatsby.* It was, he said, a triumph of realism, a highly reliable "picture book" of "the world of Long Island." Fitzgerald had captured "the exact big mansion and the flow of guests and the riotous hospitality"—even "the Ash heap off Flushing." The background of this novel, Leslie concluded, "is real."[2] Shane Leslie was a connoisseur of America and particularly of Long Island. In an account of his travels, *American Wonderland,* he later wrote about money and the Creation on Long Island: "Millionaires arrived, importing their own soil and gardens, and even their ancestral trees. Nice elm avenues arrived by lorry, and the oldest yew on the Island was transported wholesale to the lawn of a friend of mine, where it died of nostalgia. Over a hundred miles of this barren, fishlike island absorbed wealth. Thousands of smart country houses grew mushroom-like out of artificial glades and manufactured sward."[3] More than estates were being manufactured: in effect, a new American history could be created in twenty-four hours, an illusion of ancestry long in the land. Leslie's letter added, however, that there was more than the spirit of place to the novel—it was only the background that was real. The rest was what Fitzgerald had done with reality. "Real" time, place and probability are only part of the story.

In the first chapter of *The Great Gatsby* Tom Buchanan, imitating the discourse of newsstand philosophers, says that "Civilization's going to pieces" (14). He may not know the difference. But the text, in its dislocation of time and place, implies that he is right, even if not in the way he thinks. There is that great Midwestern city, San Francisco, where the ancestral Gatsbys have lived from time immemorial, or for the thirty

41

seconds or so that it takes to place them there. There is Versailles on 158th Street, the Merton College Library on West Egg, and Trinity Quad at Oggsford. Geography has many cunning corridors: the most bewildered character in the book is named Miss Baedeker. After five or six cocktails, she has the powers of the Sibyl and tells Dr. Webster Civet, who does not fear death by drowning, about the horrors of getting your head stuck in a pool. He advises her to change her life, but next year, "up in Maine" (49), he will stop prescribing. Miss Baedeker leaves the text screaming about death in New Jersey.

Gatsby's mansion "was a factual imitation of some Hôtel de Ville in Normandy, with a tower on one side, spanking new under a thin beard of raw ivy" (8). Twice disguised, it becomes later (Klipspringer plays the music that informs us) The Love Nest. Tom's house "belonged to Demaine the oil man" (10), which is to say that it comes from a vanished demesne. Nick thinks of the brewer who died of disappointment because America was not Europe, and Jordan soothes Tom's *Angst* by saying that he "ought to live in California" (14). Everywhere is somewhere else.

Fitzgerald uses a tremendous amount of factual imitation. Daisy's tour of Gatsby's house and grounds begins with the sight of a "feudal silhouette against the sky" (71), which suggests the unreal feelings of romance, of chivalry misunderstood. Gatsby belongs in that perspective—"Handsome to look at and a perfect gentleman" (57), he is a translated form of *sans peur et sans reproche*. The tour is history, but history as a dislocation of time, place, and meaning. First there are "the Marie Antoinette music rooms" (71), which connect Gatsby to the fatality of style. Myrtle Wilson will later be briefly incarnated in Marie-Antoinette both stylistically and typologically. The tour continues with Daisy, Nick, and Gatsby walking through "Restoration salons" and the Gothic "Merton College Library." Then, a progress through "period bedrooms" into "an Adam study" (72) where hospitality takes the form of a glass of Chartreuse. It is an odd drink for the moment, even in Prohibition—something else out of place, except, perhaps, for color. In Gatsby's room there are shirts sent, in high Edwardian style, by "a man in England" (72) in every color in the world, not excepting Indian blue. There are five centuries on one page and three continents and many illusions.[4] The "progress" on this tour from one time and place to another is surreal. It is not only that history has been conflated in the peculiar way that American democracy thinks of the past, but that times and places have no fixed sequence or identity. History may be as indeterminate as biography.

There is an intended disorder of depiction. Nick comes from the eternal Middle West, from a family or "clan" with a splendid "tradition" of ducal origins. But this too is fake feudalism: the family rose from a man who sent a substitute to the Civil War and then flourished in hardware by being hard-boiled. All of the places mentioned in the first chapter exist but not quite in the way usually discerned. The theme of Manifest Destiny is sounded but tells us now not to go West but in the opposite direction. And to sell bonds when we get there. Having arrived, we are in "one of the strangest communities in North America" (7). It is laboriously placed. Long Island is "due east of New York." It has certain "unusual formations of land" which have an observable "contour." They differ in every way except "shape" and "size" (8). The information seems excessive and because of that draws our attention. Is all of this geography really going to matter in the story? At this point, early in the first chapter where the scene is set, nothing seems to be figurative. We find ourselves located somewhere "in North America" and within "the Western Hemisphere" (7). The narrative begins with an actualization of place and name, with a kind of formal certainty. But within a page of this precise mapping of location, we find out that we don't know where we are, among old friends scarcely known at all.

Looking ahead for a moment, we see that the language of the narrative is quite verbally active, full of the movement of walking, running, sailing, driving, even of jumping and balancing. Everyone is (in more than one sense of the term) *going* somewhere. The impression is sometimes ("their dresses were rippling and fluttering as if they had just been blown back in after a short flight around the house" [10]) of almost magical *kinesis*. "With fenders spread like wings" (54), Nick says, "we scattered light through half Astoria." The correlatives of movement, like mobility and change, can be said to be the story itself. But the text will also state breakdown between act and thought, movement and meaning, intention and consequence. Look, for example, at the entropy of the text when it describes the Buchanans' pilgrimage from Chicago to

New York to France and back to New York again. It is described as a "drift" (9) (the term is repeated) which is the opposite of navigation. It has moral and psychological meanings. A language of kinetic exhaustion covers arrival, journey, and departure—and also character, intention, and style.[5] Tom and Daisy have lived in France "for no particular reason." They have "drifted here and there unrestfully" (9), clumping together like jellyfish wherever people "were rich together." Here and elsewhere in the text Tom and Daisy impart a sense of mechanism, that is, of subject becoming object. We are introduced to the concept early, when we see the very-nearly independent functioning of the parts of Tom's body, the ascription of will but not intelligence to them. The impression is reinforced when we see how he absorbs ideas as through a funnel, and when he himself describes his clockwork ("Once in a while I go off on a spree" [102–3]) mating routine. These people are in motion, but what they do should not be confused with action. They are adrift in terms of several kinds of transitions, including those between moral infancy and maturity.

Fitzgerald uses the term "drift" once more to describe Tom's undirected mentality; and even that enormous lawn, the color of money, comes "drifting" up to his house as if exhausted from its run up from the beach. The language of this novel is intentionally oppositional: it begins with "the Columbus story" (8) and ends with the Dutch sailors seeing Paradise regained. That is to say, it is framed by other stories of action sustained by purpose. In fact, these stories that introduce and end the narrative are full of heroic purpose. It is understood that they provide a language of intention. But when that language is applied to the protagonists, especially in terms of navigation and maneuver, it describes currents and roads and journeys going nowhere. The largest and most powerful of such descriptions comes at the end: a body touched by leaves revolves slowly, "tracing, like the leg of a compass, a thin red circle in the water" (126). It is moving, but going nowhere.[6]

The first half-dozen pages of the novel are an atlas of impressions: the Middle West and Buccleuch and New Haven and the Teutonic migration and the East and the Western hemisphere, North America and New York. Nick has a Finnish servant; Gatsby's house is Norman-French; Tom's (a different kind of illusion about time, place, and self) is Georgian Colonial.[7] There has been more than one Teutonic migration: "This idea is that we're Nordics. I am and you are and you are and—" (14). We know who we are (philosophically almost impossible) but where are we? Jordan is enroute from Asheville and Hot Springs and Palm Beach to Westchester. Nick is engaged to a girl "out West" while "Tom's got some woman in New York" (15). But Nick is not engaged, and Myrtle lives captive in the valley of ashes.

A sizable essay might be written identifying locations in *The Great Gatsby,* trying to explain movement between them as the record of a cosmopolitan decade. Place gives the story historicity. The mapping-out of so many places allows us to see the story, even to chart it according to the very landmarks of realism. Yet the geography of this novel reminds us more of *The Waste Land* than it does Rand McNally. Eliot wrote how much he liked *The Great Gatsby* after having read it "three times."[8] The first reading was probably a moment of self-recognition: there is not only the valley of ashes and the throbbing taxicab and the old Hotel Metropole but the same sense of an unreal city at the violet hour. Fitzgerald's story crosses a river from time to time and place to place. It is not the only quest for the Grail in 1922.

We remember a minor character saying gravely somewhere in the middle of the story that there are many "good roads around here" (79). But movement on them has not much to do with design and is often accidental. Throughout the novel, there will be a strange relationship between facts and certainties. The geography of *The Great Gatsby* is insistently stated—few other works of fiction locate themselves so firmly among so many identified places. That leads to certitude, and we expect the norms of realism to apply: to get from place to place according to the map—and also from inference to conclusion. But place itself becomes imponderable, and relationships between people and places become a test of those philosophical certainties that Tom Buchanan is full of, and that readers conventionally bring to texts. For example, Daisy is from Louisville and Tom is from Chicago. They marry at the Seelbach Hotel (the text is, necessarily, packed full of hotels) and go to "the South Seas" (61) for their honeymoon.[9] Later Tom asks in another hotel whether Daisy really loved him (she says no) at Kapiolani. When did or does the lie occur? Or is it a lie? Or is his question simply too stupid to expect the truth? The scene dissolves into accusations over Chicago and New Jersey. In another rented room Myrtle's traveled sister Catherine talks about Monte Carlo: "God, how I hated that town!" (29). Between her complaint and Mrs. McKee's remembrance of love safely aborted Nick has one of his many planetary meditations: "The late afternoon sky bloomed in the window for a moment like the blue honey of the Mediterranean" (29). Is it a sound if no one hears it? Was it a place if it remains unseen? If Monte Carlo (another patch of lost Eden in the text) appears then even Biloxi has its moment. A crazy quilt of logic is woven around "Blocks" Biloxi, who made boxes in Biloxi, Tennessee (there is no Biloxi, Tennessee), and who fainted at the wedding in Louisville before bride and groom left for Hawaii, and whose cousin was Bill Biloxi from Memphis (Biloxi is best known, if the phrase can be rightly used, for being in Mississippi). Biloxi was a friend of Daisy's ("I'd never seen him before" [100]) and president of Tom's class at Yale. There are no class presidents at Yale. As Tom sees it, Biloxi got to Yale about the same time that Gatsby went to Oxford. The line that follows, about "Mr. Nobody from Nowhere" (101), seems to have a much wider application than even Tom suspects.[10]

At this distance from the publication of the text a certain amount of archaeology is needed to get on the same level as the original audience. We are attuned to the presence of myth and even of epic in *The Great Gatsby,* and we can sense its powers of allusion. But the spirit of place is conveyed also by lyric. Here is one of the many points in the narrative where it is intersected by words and music that become part of its own text:

> For Daisy was young and her artificial world was redolent of orchids and pleasant, cheerful snobbery and orchestras which set the rhythm of the year, summing up the sadness and suggestiveness of life in new tunes. All night the saxophones wailed the hopeless comment of the "Beale Street Blues" while a hundred pairs of golden and silver slippers shuffled the shining dust. At the grey tea hour there were always rooms that throbbed incessantly with this low sweet fever, while fresh faces drifted here and there like rose petals blown by the sad horns around the floor.

Through this twilight universe Daisy began to move again with
the season. (118)

Fitzgerald made this passage do double duty: it was cannibalized from
"Diamond Dick and the First Law of Woman" in *Hearst's International
Magazine* of April 1924.[11] *Beale Street Blues* became, I think, a theme song
for Daisy. We have seen the Goddess before and know her now in this
incarnation. That phrase "to move again with the season" is intended
to be a warning: love is morally neutral and the annual sequence of
things is predictive of both love and death. But there is something else,
a counterpoint to the "rhythm of the year" and to the harmonic music
of the spheres. This "low sweet fever" is about a certain place and definitely about a state of mind. *Beale Street Blues* (lyrics and music by W. C.
Handy, 1916) is set in Memphis and brings to its white audience feelings best expressed by black music.

Fitzgerald wrote that before jazz was music it was dancing, and before it was dancing it was sex.[12] Daisy may come from Louisville but
she thinks Memphis. "If Beale Street could talk," W. C. Handy wrote,
"Married men would have to take their beds and walk."[13] Its women
are for sale ("pretty Browns, in beautiful gowns"), and they drive men
crazy. The audience of 1925, which did not have to look up words and
music, may have felt the resonance of the line, "bus'ness never closes
til somebody gets killed." The "sad horns" described by Nick are a jazz
elegy. "If Beale Street could talk" (the line precipitates what we hope is
the meaning of literary criticism), it would tell us why place is idea:

> I've seen the lights of gay Broadway,
> Old Market Street down by the Frisco Bay,
> I've strolled the Prado,
> I've gambled on the Bourse
> The seven wonders of the world I've seen
> And many are the places I have been.

This is the way Daisy feels, or thinks of herself as feeling. Music is
character: Daisy is not complete as described—Fitzgerald could not ac-
complish that and keeps on telling us about her through gesture and
music. The famous difficulties of conceptualizing character that were

the subject of Fitzgerald's correspondence with Max Perkins were re-solved elliptically, through symbolic allusion.[14] In this case, without Daisy having to *state* or *act,* her character (in a song about women for sale) is set to music. Less concrete but more important: *Beale Street Blues* is an elegiac equivalent to the events of the narrative. I think that we are supposed to hear it or at least know in what sense it applies to the story. Fitzgerald's strategy is not to release a great deal of emotion through dialogue. The emotional release is often accompanied by—translated by—lyric and music. Gatsby does not express feeling, but he knows what it is: "Don't talk so much, old sport," commanded Gatsby. "Play!" (74). Klipspringer hears the Muse and plays about love from "morning" through "evening," from "In the meantime" to "In be-tween time——" (75). In the midst of the storm and through music, at "the hour of a profound human change," Gatsby finally speaks to Daisy about time and is understood. Music has a high degree of speci-ficity in and for the text: we hear the *Sheik of Araby* (and the line "Your love belongs to me" [62]) just before Nick begins his *affaire* with Jordan; "The Love Nest" is played when Daisy comes back to Gatsby at his house; and there are "the portentous chords of Mendelssohn's Wedding March" (99) as the argument over marriage begins at the Plaza. Music conveys meanings that evade direct statement, and it states outcomes. *The Great Gatsby* has more music in it than Caliban's island.

Time and place are suggested by dreams as well as by lyrics. Some unexpected people have dreams in this story, for example, George B. and Myrtle Wilson:

> "I've been here too long. I want to get away. My wife and I
> want to go west."
> "Your wife does!" exclaimed Tom, startled.
> "She's been talking about it for ten years." (96)

This is one dream in a text that is full of meditations, nightmares, fanta-sies, day-dreams, echoes of film and stage—and echoes of our history. The dream of the Dutch sailors at the end of the story has been first, and has diffused itself, in ways more and less faithful, into the myriad dreams of everyone else in the story—always with the exception of Jordan, who "was too wise ever to carry well-forgotten dreams from age to age" (106). Myrtle Wilson falls naturally enough into the great idea of renewal and rebirth, of going West.

Affected by the current meanings of the phrase "The American Dream," we tend to think of *The Great Gatsby* as if it were some enlarged Horatio Alger story mediated by romance. There is a powerful disposition to see the book as a photographic record of the jazz age. An equally powerful disposition persists to validate this novel primarily because it leads to us. The novel immortalizes its *present* audience because it lends credence to the idea that the freedom to do what we want and become what we want is the essential freedom. Many readers see in it the tragedy of their own expectations. But freedom and mobility are a late variant of the original dream, and Fitzgerald understood the fact perfectly. He writes here not about success or about our universal right to become what we think we are; rather he details the misunderstanding and degradation of an idea. Going West is an idea even older than America.

Perhaps the following poem, which is about sailors off the American shore, can tell us something about "the last time in history" when facts and dreams were the same:

> Where the remote *Bermudas* ride
> In th'Oceans bosome unespy'd,
> From a small Boat, that row'd along,
> The listening Winds receiv'd this Song.
> What should we do but sing his Praise
> That led us through the watry Maze. . . .
>
> He gave us this eternal Spring,
> Which here enamells every thing;
> And sends the Fowl's to us in care,
> On daily Visits through the Air.
> He hangs in shades the Orange bright,
> Like golden Lamps in a green Night. . . .
>
> Oh let our Voice his Praise exalt,
> Till it arrive at Heavens Vault:
> Which thence (perhaps) rebounding may
> Eccho beyond the *Mexique Bay*.

> Thus sung they, in the *English* boat,
> An holy and a chearful Note,
> And all the way, to guide their Chime,
> With falling Oars they kept the time.[15]

"Bermudas," by Andrew Marvell, is a hymn to the Discovery and to the Creation. It tries to tell, if art could tell, the effect of America on the historical imagination. It is not Utopian. It is deeply Puritanical—and in that respect has something to say about the residual Puritanism of Nick Carraway. The dream of the sailors, English or Dutch, is what Fitzgerald means by the "last and greatest of all human dreams" (140). Going back in history as, on the last pages of the novel he tells us we must do, we can see what that dream first meant. The New World implied the Creation as it might have been before man's Fall. It was free of history, without civilized sin. It might better fulfill the intentions of Creation than civilization had already done.

Even at our most secular we have believed in the special destiny of the New World. But the belief became ever more secular. By 1922, when *The Great Gatsby* takes place, the American Dream had little to do with Providence divine and a great deal to do with feelings organized around style and personal change—and above all, with the unexamined self. After ten years of thinking over the jazz age Fitzgerald wrote that its crucial year had in fact been 1922, "the peak of the younger generation."[16] In that year traditional values were dissolved, history forgotten, and, in 1923, "with a whoop the orgy began." Fitzgerald's analysis contained one especially interesting point, given the course of world history then: it was "characteristic of the Jazz Age that it had no interest in politics at all." I interpret that to mean that it had no interest in all those other things subsumed in American life by politics. The central irony developed by the novel is that our largest feelings, love and faith, can only be directed at objects unable to contain them. John Donne wrote in the age of exploration of his mistress as "My America, my new found lande."[17] He knew the difference, but he knew also that love for the Creation was the adequate equivalent for his feelings. In Donne, in Shakespeare's *Antony and Cleopatra,* largeness of character sustains the identity of self and world. But Nick, who thinks continually of time and space, so that we always have to find a dimension for his remarks, knows the consequences for Gatsby when he transfers "his unutterable visions to her perishable breath" (86).

The American Dream has in this story undergone a great sea-change. We have always been ready to read it as a parable of success. That is what the dream has become, not what it once was. In its modern form the dream can be seen in disguise, as Myrtle Wilson experiences it through the urgings of scandal sheets and advertisements. But the first form of the dream is stated through the Eden visions and Paradise regained visions of Gatsby and Nick. The components of such a vision are wonder at the encounter with a new reality; love greater than *eros* but expressed by it; the annihilation of the mere self. If Nick is a Puritan he is not a petty moralist but a man with a powerful and historical sensibility, alive to "the promises of life" (6) in their totality. Nick addresses many things directly in this text—for example, honor—but none more important than faith. But even the great premodern virtues have diminished: Gatsby's love is greater than his mentality and Nick's continuous debate between conscience and will becomes often a comic form of the stern self-questioning that he brings to mind.

The text is haunted by a place that is no longer there. Sometimes there is a glimpse of what the ancient exploration sought, "the scalloped ocean and the abounding blessed isles" (92). Sometimes Eden is briefly incarnated: "the city seen from the Queensboro Bridge is always the city seen for the first time, in its first wild promise of all the mystery and the beauty in the world" (55). A good Catholic education, as the phrase used to go, would even for an indifferent student like Fitzgerald have had something to say about the cities of man and God: "the earthly city . . . shall not be everlasting"—[18] part of the meaning of the novel's extraordinary preoccupation with the passing of time. There are redemptive qualities of place identified with childhood, virginity, and the eradication of desire. That is to say, only with the past:

> When we pulled out into the winter night and the real snow, our snow, began to stretch out beside us and twinkle against the windows, and the dim lights of small Wisconsin stations moved by, a sharp wild brace came suddenly into the air. We drew in deep

breaths of it as we walked back from dinner through the cold vesti-
bules, unutterably aware of our identity with this country for one
strange hour before we melted indistinguishably into it again.

That's my middle-west—not the wheat or the prairies or the
lost Swede towns but the thrilling, returning trains of my youth
and the street lamps and sleigh bells in the frosty dark and the
shadows of holly wreaths thrown by lighted windows on the snow.
I am part of that.[19] (137)

There is Louisville in 1917, with its Jacob's Ladder to "a secret place
above the trees" (86) (in Genesis the "top of it reached to heaven"
and a promise is made, "I will not leave thee"). There is the golden
palace in Crete and the innocently romantic "Araby." Jordan says, "I
love New York on summer afternoons. . . . There's something very sen-
suous about it—overripe, as if all sorts of funny fruits were going to
fall into your hands." With disconcerting frequency, this other place,
Eden, intrudes itself into mind and text. There are many things in the
restaurant in which Nick meets Wolfshiem on Forty-second Street, but
what the mind sees are its "Presbyterian nymphs on the ceiling" (56) in
their endless pastoral.[20] Wolfshiem himself invokes the old Metropole,
a place "full of memories" (56) of the blessed dead. The story proceeds
on one level, depicting time and place with the utmost precision—but
it proceeds also by contradictions of temporality.

Tom drifts and Jordan drives (on the edge of the road) and Myrtle
wants to "go west" to begin life over. From its first to its last page the
text states itself in the language of movement and of navigation. A book
that ends with the vision of the Dutch sailors in the New World tells
us of destiny in terms of charts and shallows, and its hero is seen in
his own boat resting his oars against the current. Over a great river a
funeral slowly passes carrying a dead man who has sailed from "southeastern Europe" (55) to end in this place. The language of navigation is
deeply rooted in the text—admonitory, proleptic. When we finally see
Gatsby floating in a current with "hardly the shadows of waves" (126),
both the metaphor and life have ceased. Gatsby's body traces the circle
made by a compass on a navigator's chart.

Throughout the text the cosmos moves, and time has a beat even
more formidable than the stroke of thirty. The narrative is full of watches

and clocks and schedules and calendars that set one kind of time, but life seems governed by time of a different order, by sun and tide and phases of the moon and seasons. Toward the end of the book, the two kinds of time connect superbly:

> "What'll we do with ourselves this afternoon," cried Daisy, "and the day after that, and the next thirty years?"
>
> "Don't be morbid," Jordan said, "Life starts all over again when it gets crisp in the fall."
>
> "But it's so hot," insisted Daisy, on the verge of tears. "And everything's so confused."[21] (92)

It is hot enough for the earth to fall into the sun or for Icarus to lose his wings after all. Everything is indeed confused in time and place. But that is also part of the narrative technique: so much is simultaneous, and expressed by new ideas of association, that older and more directly intelligible ways of telling a story no longer apply.

Notes

1. F. Scott Fitzgerald, "My Lost City," *The Crack-Up,* ed. Edmund Wilson (New York: New Directions, 1945), p. 27.

2. Matthew J. Bruccoli and Margaret M. Duggan, eds., *Correspondence of F. Scott Fitzgerald* (New York: Random House, 1980), p. 174.

3. Shane Leslie, *American Wonderland* (London: Michael Joseph, 1936), p. 43.

4. For a review of interpretations of this passage see Kent Cartwright, "Nick Carraway as an Unreliable Narrator," *Papers on Language and Literature* 20, no. 2 (Spring 1984): 225. Cartwright notes that the tour shows "incongruent riches" but does not deal with Gatsby's manufactured history; and he sees the house simply as a "fairyland" of materialism.

5. See M. A. Klug, "Horns of Manichaeus: The Conflict of Art and Experience in *The Great Gatsby* and *The Sun Also Rises,*" *Essays in Literature* 12, no. 1 (Spring 1985): 113. For a discussion of "phrases and images . . . which centre on words like *restless* and *drifting,*" see W. J. Harvey, "Theme and Texture in *The Great Gatsby*" in *Critical Essays on F. Scott Fitzgerald's The Great Gatsby,* ed. Scott Donaldson (Boston: G. K. Hall, 1984), pp. 83–84. For the connection of the idea of "drift" to the "manners" of life in this cultural moment, see Milton R. Stern, *The Golden Moment: The Novels of F. Scott Fitzgerald* (Urbana: University of Illinois Press, 1970), pp. 199–200.

6. The scene is one of several in the novel with specifically visual quality. There is no dialogue, and such scenes may refer themselves to still and motion-picture photography. All are intensely concerned with the details of perception; all are silent on meaning and morality. It is as if (in accordance with modernist practice and assumptions) a decision has been made to be expressive only through form. See the brief discussion of form by Malcolm Bradbury, "The Cities of Modernism," in *Modernism*, ed. Bradbury and James McFarlane (New York: Penguin, 1983), p. 100.

7. "Colonial" design came to mean a great deal for industrial (and personal) imitation. See Miles Orvell, *The Real Thing: Imitation and Authenticity in American Culture, 1880–1940* (Chapel Hill: University of North Carolina Press, 1989), p. 167: In 1927

> Rockefeller agreed to finance the restoration of Colonial Williamsburg. And it was symptomatic of the period's ambivalence in the face of radical change that the backward-looking impulse could coexist with an equal and opposite enthusiasm for the machine, as if the one could balance the other. Thus an implicit rejection of modernity was evident in the widespread middle-class enthusiasm for imitation Colonial furniture and architecture. Made first for the mass market in the 1880s and going strong through the 1920s, the colonial style offered a comforting security in the face of rapid change.

Houses and antiques became political statements in the age of undesired mass immigration. In fact, colonial relics became "a symbol of old and glorious spiritual and political values, now lost in an age of mongrel designs." Orvell suggests that possession of images of the past was understood to offset social change; to establish a "colonial" family claim through consumption. He observes that in the late twenties Henry Ford was the most notable colonialist, completely recreating the vanished order of the past in his Dearborn preindustrial museum.

8. Fitzgerald, *The Crack-Up*, p. 310.

9. See Matthew J. Bruccoli, *Apparatus for F. Scott Fitzgerald's the Great Gatsby [Under the Red, White, and Blue]* (Columbia, South Carolina: University of South Carolina Press, 1974), p. 42, for the many names (Muhlbach, Seelbach, Muehlebach, Sealbach) of this hotel in the text.

10. See the witty discussion of the Biloxi passage in Arnold Weinstein's "Fiction as Greatness: The Case of Gatsby," *Novel* 19, no. 1 (Fall 1985): 33–35. "Blocks" Biloxi is a product of "collective fabulation"—each person discussing him contributes some false fact to his biography. By the end of the conversation at the Plaza Biloxi has wound up as a mysterious "image" of Gatsby, the self-made man whose life has also been manufactured.

11. "Diamond Dick and the First Law of Woman" is reprinted in *The Price*

Was High, ed. Matthew J. Bruccoli (New York: Harcourt Brace Jovanovich, 1979), pp. 69–85.

12. Fitzgerald, "Echoes of the Jazz Age," *The Crack-Up,* p. 16.

13. W. C. Handy, *A Treasury of the Blues* (New York: Charles Boni, 1949), pp. 102–5.

14. Fitzgerald acknowledged the difficulty of putting conceptions about character into description. He thought that Tom, Myrtle, and Gatsby were successfully drawn as envisioned but that Daisy and Jordan had eluded him: "I'm sorry Myrtle is better than Daisy. Jordan of course was a great idea (perhaps you know its Edith Cummings) but she fades out." From John Kuehl and Jackson R. Bryer, eds., *Dear Scott/Dear Max: The Fitzgerald-Perkins Correspondence* (New York: Charles Scribner's Sons, 1971), p. 90.

15. Andrew Marvell, "Bermudas," in *The Poems & Letters of Andrew Marvell,* ed. H. M. Margoliouth, 2 vols. (Oxford: Oxford University Press, 1952), 2:17–18.

16. Fitzgerald, "Echoes of the Jazz Age," *The Crack-Up,* p. 15.

17. John Donne, "To his Mistris Going to Bed," in *The Elegies And the Songs And Sonnets,* ed. Helen Gardner (Oxford: Clarendon Press, 1965), p. 15.

18. Saint Augustine, *The City of God,* trans. Marcus Dods (New York: Modern Library, 1950), p. 480. The passage is also a Protestant *locus classicus:* it occurs between the discussion of Genesis and of the origin of secular history. See Peter Brown, *Augustine of Hippo* (Berkeley: University of California Press, 1969), pp. 313f.

19. Fitzgerald left the realism of those "lost Swede towns" to Sinclair Lewis and Willa Cather. The following description of a midwestern Swedish town is from the 1929 edition of *O Pioneers* (Boston: Houghton Mifflin), pp. 3–4:

> . . . Low drab buildings huddled on the gray prairie, under a gray sky. The dwelling-houses were set about haphazard as if they had been moved in overnight. . . . None of them had any appearance of permanence, and the howling wind blew under them as well as over them. The main street was a deeply rutted road, now frozen hard, which ran from the squat red railway station and the grain 'elevator' at the north end of the town to the lumber yard and the horse pond at the south end.

See Tom Quirk, "Fitzgerald and Cather: *The Great Gatsby,*" *American Literature* 54, no. 4 (December 1982): 576f. Fitzgerald did not use Cather's realistic detail but he may have been influenced by her narrative of social change and change of character.

20. See Bruccoli, *Apparatus,* pp. 40–41, for the spelling of Wolfshiem/Wolfsheim.

21. Daisy's lines echo *The Waste Land:* "What shall we do to-morrow?/ What shall we ever do?"

3

The Marketplace

■ The second chapter of *The Great Gatsby*, about Versailles at 158th Street, is one of the most intentional sequences in fiction since Balzac to describe the urban world in terms of transaction, style, and change. To understand this accomplishment we have to understand advertising and other instructions for acquired selves. The novel was written by a former copywriter for the Barron Collier agency and appeared at roughly the same time as the first issue of the *New Yorker*. It understands thoroughly the meaning of R. H. Macy's claim to sell "Goods suitable for the millionaire, at prices in reach of the millions."[1]

Business and especially advertising history bears out André Le Vot's claim that Fitzgerald's work is connected to the "revolution in manners" after the war.[2] The marketplace considered itself to be revolutionary. Advertising theory was primitive in the early twenties, but it was beginning to make claims about the reasons why things sold. Here is what an industry text had to say in 1928 about the course of Fitzgerald's lifetime:

> The changes in consumption are not easy to measure accurately, but it may be worth while to address ourselves to certain of them which have been conspicuous during this first quarter of the twentieth century.
>
> The population of the United States since 1900 has increased 40%. In contrast with this the following facts are worth keeping in mind:
>
> The wealth per capita is four times as great as in 1900
>
> Farm values are over three times as great
>
> Bank deposits are over six times as great
>
> Bank clearings are over four times as great.
>
> In other words, each of these evidences of individual or social wealth with their indirect inflections of increased consumption of consumer goods has expanded at a much more rapid rate than has the population.[3]

It was a dream fulfilled for the advertising industry, which began its symbiotic relationship with automobiles and movies. The former were its main product, taking up most of the space in layouts; the latter brought the advantages of the "Star" system to the display of new styles. In the movies glamour was a function not entirely of sex but of designer furnishings and slinky clothing—national styles began to originate on screen, as when Gloria Swanson dazzled the world in her bath wardrobe, and when *Flaming Youth* could show the full implications of bobbed hair.[4] It did not take the advertising industry long to realize that it was no longer in the business of retailing commodities. It now sold ideas about selves. Fully conscious of their new power, advertising men and women wrote a good many books and essays on their mission. Part of that was also new: although advertising had had a tremendous start in the late nineteenth century it never really coped with the idea of urging change in order to increase the circulation of goods and services. After the war, however, goods and services were no longer thought of as necessities but in terms of created demand.[5] The satirical opening pages of Fitzgerald's short story "May Day" are about the spoils of "peace and prosperity," which are "hymned by the scribes and poets" of consumption. As this story begins—and as the decade begins—the two great social orders that Fitzgerald sees are those of "spenders" and "merchants."[6]

The advertising revolution had more to it than increased Gross National Product and enlarged personal wealth. Consumer industries absorbed not only the idea that demand could be created but that it could be paid for on credit. And, most important, that style and utility were not the same. Style became associated with change. Le Vot's biography of Fitzgerald describes those products that generated the energies of sales and also of fiction. Many of them were cosmetic (we see a world of cosmetic profusion in those disguising things "unguent, powdered, or liquid" in *The Waste Land*). Myrtle's acquisition of cold cream and perfume, her drug-store life-style, are visible evidence for the boom in beauty—an industry built not only around the idea of self-improvement but also on that of self-change.

Here is advice on something more serious from a copy writer in 1925: "data must be revised often these days. In the past few years radical changes in wealth and social status, which always affect women more decidedly than men, have occurred and must continue to occur. The changes are taking place so rapidly, that even to-morrow may be different from to-day. . . . You can advertise to fifteen-year-old flappers to-day, whereas ten or twenty years ago, fifteen-year-olds were still in the nursery, more or less!"[7] There seems not to be much of a moral imperative—sexual opportunity is quietly noted, with a certain nervous satisfaction—but there is full awareness of the relationship of sales to social change, and especially of the new status of women in the marketplace.

The "revolution," led by Coco Chanel, was in the process of democratizing style. It took only one yard of material for a Chanel dress, and that might be a cheap synthetic like rayon. Design would suggest sexual and other kinds of freedom, especially freedom from the constraints of middle-class life. Over the decade the new style prevailed and women changed, as Le Vot puts it, from looking like violins to looking like clarinets. The change was not easy to assimilate: even a modernist like William Carlos Williams thought that Nancy Cunard, a representative figure in every sense of the term, was "straight as any stick" and even "emaciated." Another observer of the new style thought she looked "like an asparagus."[8] In *The Great Gatsby* Jordan Baker's style is androgynous—she is described as if she were a Brancusi with "clean, hard" lines. The overtones are more than stylistic, as in comparable descriptions by Waugh and Hemingway.[9]

But the marketplace was still in 1922 divided into opposed sectors. Myrtle Wilson chooses to imitate old money rather than new style. Her dress is, to use Nick's word for it, "elaborate." It follows a style that uses many yards of material for each piece. The style calls for heavy use of ornament and complication. It calls for changing dresses at appropriate hours of the day. When Myrtle models that style in her apartment—and she is supremely aware of the relationship of that style to her new self—she displays more than clothes.

Nature and Fitzgerald have made Myrtle Wilson full-breasted, fleshy, stout, almost exaggeratedly Edwardian. She dresses in yards of chiffon, which help her to imitate high society, not café society. Is there some special personal meaning in her style for Tom? Or does he simply have a taste for chambermaids? His argument with the modern world is objectified by women. Myrtle is, like his own ideas, old-fashioned. She seems to be an antidote for modern times. Myrtle is socially subordinate, from a class long used to provide mistresses. She is kept, which is to say that the relationship is not only a replication of class sexual relations *but of ideal domestic life*. Tom wants another milieu, with a woman waiting in an apartment for him. Her style acknowledges his condition.

Not for Myrtle the appearance of modernism. A good recent history of fashion makes the point: "modernist painting was about abstract light, space and colour. In the 1920s fashionable dress simply imitated this angular, two-dimensional style."[10] The "fashion nihilism" of Chanel and the "surrealism" of Schiaparelli had sexual and social equivalents.[11] But Myrtle's appearance suggests her acquiescence to Tom's ideas about the good life, as well as her own. She does not want to look like Coco Chanel; she wants to look like Mrs. Astor.

Myrtle lives in a domestic world that has been previously invented by magazines.[12] Some of them are scattered all over her apartment, and her apartment embodies what they have to say about the good life of acquisition. It will take a long time—several pages in the text of a very short novel—for Nick adequately to describe the goods in it, and the services:

> "My dear," she told her sister in a high mincing shout, "most of these fellas will cheat you every time. All they think of is money. I had a woman up here last week to look at my feet and when she gave me the bill you'd of thought she had my appendicitus out."
> "What was the name of the woman?" asked Mrs. McKee.
> "Mrs. Eberhardt. She goes around looking at people's feet in their own homes." (27)

This is more than an anecdote of traveling podiatry. Mrs. Eberhardt's *persona* comes floating into a story in which all the characters and many ideas are perceived through passage. But she has a larger role to play, as part of the marketplace milieu in which anything can be sold, and in which transaction is relationship. Myrtle is right in her two assumptions that anything can be bought and everyone will cheat you. There are not many limits to acquisition: those "finest specimens of human molars" (57), which are Wolfshiem's cufflinks, illustrate more than eccentricity. Nick looks at them and says, with unconscious percipience, "That's a very interesting idea."

Fernand Braudel, the historian of daily life, has devoted a large part of his work to fashion and style. According to Braudel, "the study of things" is the truest historical essential.[13] Things—furniture, hangings, changing styles of clothes, or the act of changing clothes—constitute material reality. In Fitzgerald things are more than elements of description. Certain characters are aggregates of things while certain things are more than material. There are suits and dresses to buy, and shirts to display, and ash trays and cars and perfumes to state their significance for life. From the first we know that use is not a criterion. If it were, then no one would cry over shirts with stripes and scrolls and plaids in coral and apple-green and lavender and faint orange. Here is Myrtle Wilson in pursuit of an idea:

> At the news-stand she bought a copy of "Town Tattle" and a moving picture magazine and, in the station drug store, some cold cream and a small flask of perfume. Upstairs in the solemn echoing drive she let four taxi cabs drive away before she selected a new one, lavender-colored with grey upholstery, and in this we slid out from the mass of the station into the glowing sunshine. But immediately she turned sharply from the window and leaning forward tapped on the front glass.
>
> "I want to get one of those dogs," she said earnestly. "I want to get one for the apartment. They're nice to have—a dog." (23–24)

Myrtle's lines, which break down metrically, are even for her unusually flat-footed. They call attention to themselves because of the framing of Nick's description. There are only three verbs Myrtle uses to describe her acquisition, and they are very different from those used by Nick. She repeats the elemental marketplace phrases "want," "get," and "have." They are the operative phrases of consumer society, their *lingua franca*. There are important differences also in the level of mental energy. Myrtle can be compared to Nick, and not to her disadvantage, in the directness of her prose, in her active will.

Myrtle does not trip herself up by claiming that what she wants is either new or good. Nothing in the novel indicates that dogs mean anything to her. And yet moment and choice are important: "I'd like to get one of those police dogs; I don't suppose you got that kind?" (24). That "police dog" has been conjured up not out of childhood memory or adult loneliness but out of pure and disinterested *gestalt*, "for the apartment." It is momentarily existent in the text because it is momentarily existent in Myrtle's mind; a residue of instructions she has filed away. She knows something with a hard and limited intelligence, that objects take the place of thoughts and become part of selves.[14] The dog makes the apartment and Myrtle complete, exactly as she has seen matron and pet in advertisements. Myrtle is neither stupid nor inarticulate; and she is not displaying the mania of impulse-buying. What she does is the opposite of buying by impulse; it is buying according to plan.[15]

Myrtle's acquisitions are more than clothes and furniture and images of the good bourgeois life. That self-classifying phrase, "My dear," means as much to her as "old sport" does to Gatsby. She has bought and paid for it—it comes from magazines and gossip-columns and advertisements that offer advice on mobility. It has almost certainly come from movies, which from the early twenties on tried to raise the social tone of the industry by depicting life among the rich and fashionable.[16] Equally important, the movie industry tried to accommodate to a new audience, to produce the modern equivalent of conduct books for it. There was an entire genre of film for shopgirls who dreamt of "the social circles of the rich, and sought a knowledge of table etiquette, how to dress, how to be introduced, how to order, and how to conduct oneself in general."[17] Myrtle's pet phrase is meant to be seen alongside Gatsby's. When he uses his phrase one time too many, when he insists on the reality of his acquired identity, Tom Buchanan becomes much more upset than when he finds out that Daisy is having an affair. He very nearly goes over the edge, and yells, "Don't you call me 'old sport'!" (105). Chaplin caught this sensation when he dressed the Little Tramp in remnants of gentility. His clothes mimic the aspirations of his audience.

Myrtle's falling in love with Tom is unforgettable for her and should be for us: "He had on a dress suit and patent leather shoes and I couldn't keep my eyes off him but every time he looked at me I had to pretend to be looking at the advertisement over his head" (31). Her recollection is itself framed by the strip of ads running over windows and doors. We are forced by the prose that Fitzgerald uses to recognize Myrtle's own natural sense of their connection to her feelings. Is it too much to say that her feelings respond to images and commodities? The first time after her marriage that she cries is when she finds out that her husband had to borrow a suit for the ceremony. Braudel asks, "Is fashion in fact such a trifling thing? Or is it, as I prefer to think, rather an indication of deeper phenomena—of the energies, possibilities, demands and *joie de vivre* of a given society, economy and civilization?"[18] Fashion may even be, he adds, "a search for a new language." Myrtle cries over Wilson's suit; Daisy cries over Gatsby's shirts—things evidently are correlatives for ideas, as translatable as if they themselves were elements of language.

We don't want to lose track of what Braudel calls the "energies" of style and the psychological "demands" to which it responds. On the way to Myrtle's Little Trianon Nick says that the day was so pastoral that he wouldn't have been surprised "to see a great flock of white sheep turn the corner" (25). The allusion is structural: their Marie-Antoinette throws a completely "regal" glance round the neighborhood before entering her wedding-cake of a building. She takes possession "haughtily" (hauteur, according to the Oxford English Dictionary, is a royal quality) of a kingdom of things. They are also things of a kingdom:

> The living room was crowded to the doors with a set of tapestried furniture entirely too large for it so that to move about was to stumble continually over scenes of ladies swinging in the gardens of Versailles. The only picture was an over-enlarged photograph, apparently a hen sitting on a blurred rock. Looked at from a distance however the hen resolved itself into a bonnet and the countenance of a stout old lady beamed down into the room. Several old copies of "Town Tattle" lay on the table together with a copy of "Simon Called Peter," and some of the small scandal magazines of Broadway. (25)

In addition to the above there are a dog with its box and straw; milk and biscuits; whiskey and cigarettes; "innumerable" pottery bracelets jangling on the arms of Myrtle's multichrome sister Catherine; an elaborate afternoon dress of cream colored chiffon; and drinks, ice, mineral water. There is good reason for Nick, after seeing all these things, to be "simultaneously enchanted and repelled by the inexhaustible variety of life" (30) by the plenitude of object and being. The scene is a phenomenology of industrial life.[19]

When Nick makes that remark he is thinking of the city below but it applies to the microcosm of the apartment. Here, on the inside, "inexhaustible variety" describes not only personality but also the infinity of modes by which it asserts itself. Each of the beings in this place has become visible through its connection to things: Catherine can be heard before she is seen; and even the dog settles into its brief existence surrounded by the artifacts of doggy distinction. But things and meanings are disconnected. The scene dissolves first into drunkenness and then into reverie and finally into unrestful sleep. The last collection of things we see is a portfolio of fake art: "Beauty and the Beast . . . Loneliness . . . Old Grocery Horse . . . Brook'n Bridge" (32). There may be a plenum of things in this inexhaustible world but they seem to have the same kind of relationship to meaning that McKee's photos have to art.

McKee's photos represent "creative temperament," otherwise known to Nick and to the reader as "flabby impressionability" (6) Both terms, mentioned as the novel begins, will turn out to have defining powers. The appearance of a fake artist so early in the story indicates that Fitzgerald wants to draw out the two apparently opposed meanings. McKee is one of several characters in the book ("A grey old man who bore an absurd resemblance to John D. Rockefeller" is another [24]) who are in the business of selling ideas. If you want a police dog, then it's a police dog; if you want Myrtle as Mrs. Astor then only a little camera work remains. Endowed almost allegorically with fake creativity, McKee sums up one other important function: he reminds us of how feelings and ideas are produced and circulate in mass society. At this early moment in the narrative Fitzgerald establishes the skepticism necessary to judge claims about the expression of feeling. McKee imitates the imitation of reality of Norman Rockwell and Coles Phillips but misses the richness of their ideas and of their ideologies.[20] If his craft is realism, and if he has novelistic equivalents, then more than one craft may have to be reinvented.

Most of the products consumed by Myrtle are imitations, even that "police" dog whose genealogy is a function of supply and demand. There are moments in the text devoted to sales and salestalk, but none so illustrative as the answer to Myrtle's question, "What kind are they?":

> The man peered doubtfully into the basket, plunged in his hand and drew one up, wriggling, by the back of the neck.
> "That's no police dog," said Tom.

"No, it's not exactly a pol*ice* dog," said the man with disappointment in his voice. "It's more of an airedale."

Confusions of identity—airedale or police dog, "boy" or "girl," dog or bitch—respond to the main issues. Myrtle is now in her new identity talking to a vendor who not only resembles but represents John D. Rockefeller. The dog is worth a fortune but costs ten dollars, that is, the amount of money needed to get ten more. As Nick says later on about New York, one gets the feeling that anything is possible—can Standard Oil be running an assembly line of "very recent" mutts at an eye-popping profit of a thousand percent? Clearly an impossible thought, but a small circle is completed when, later in the story, Gatsby says, "I was in the oil business" (71). The same principles, as Myrtle has told the reader and Mrs. McKee, apply everywhere. Gatsby, Rockefeller, and "Demaine the oil man" (10) are entwined in their enterprise.

In Myrtle's world everyone uses the same commodities under the impression that they confer uniqueness. Those "tapestry scenes" replicate Versailles, which is the only thing in the world like itself. What matters is not the transparent falsity of the claim to reproduce the original. Tocqueville made this connection between commodities and social change: "if one finds quantities of things generally shoddy and very cheap, one can be sure that in that country privilege is on the wane and classes are beginning to mix and will soon lose their identity."[21] Fitzgerald's story takes place when power is passing from old to new money, with consequences for all forms of public and private life. Tom will have anxieties about social change while Myrtle will try to take advantage of it. In such circumstances the marketplace becomes increasingly active. Eventually, Tocqueville says, it begins to sell meanings: "Craftsmen in democratic ages do not seek only to bring the useful things they make within the reach of every citizen, but also try to give each object a look of brilliance unconnected with its true worth." As for the consumer, "In the confusion of classes each man wants to appear as something he is not and is prepared to take much trouble to produce this effect. Such feelings are not born of democracy, for they are all too natural to the heart of man, but it is democracy which applies them to material products."

To bring the matter up to date, Daniel Boorstin writes that it was in the mid-twenties that the relationship of appearance and "material objects" took on its modern form: the object itself began to matter less than the impression it made on the buyer. The pioneer study of advertising *Packages That Sell* by Richard Franken and Carroll Larrabee (1928) identified 1925 as the crucial period for marketing in America: it was then that advertising really learned, through packaging and picturing, "to create a desire in the consumer's mind."[22]

When Myrtle Wilson mentions "all the things I got to do" (31) she means all the things "I've got to get." Her agenda: "A massage and a wave and a collar for the dog and one of those cute little ash trays where you touch a spring, and a wreath with a black silk bow for mother's grave that'll last all summer" (31). Her list has been created in advance and anticipates satisfaction. She carefully says that she wants "one of those" ash trays, a known commodity with its own relationship to her own sense of fulfillment.

As the party begins we see that Myrtle has changed and is now "attired in an elaborate afternoon dress of cream colored chiffon which gave out a continual rustle as she swept about the room" (26). Nick understands that the change of dress has caused a change of identity: "With the influence of the dress her personality had also undergone a change. The intense vitality that had been so remarkable in the garage was converted into impressive hauteur" (26). The connection is emphatic between "attired" and "converted."

Myrtle, Mrs. McKee, and Chester go into the most extensive transaction of the novel: Myrtle wants to look as if she belongs with Tom inherently; Mrs. McKee wants to broker the exchange between art and social character; and Chester wants badly to get all this down on film so that he can finally get to sell something on the North Shore:

> "I like your dress," remarked Mrs. McKee. "I think it's adorable."
>
> Mrs. Wilson rejected the compliment by raising her eyebrow in disdain.
>
> "It's just a crazy old thing," she said. "I just slip it on sometimes when I don't care what I look like."
>
> "But it looks wonderful on you, if you know what I mean,"

pursued Mrs. McKee. "If Chester could only get you in that pose
I think he could make something of it."

We all looked in silence at Mrs. Wilson who removed a strand
of hair from over her eyes and looked back at us with a brilliant
smile. Mr. McKee regarded her intently with his head on one side
and then moved his hand back and forth slowly in front of his face.

"I should change the light," he said after a moment. "I'd like to
bring out the modelling of the features. And I'd try to get hold of
all the back hair."

"I wouldn't think of changing the light," cried Mrs. McKee. "I
think it's——." (27)

One key phrase is the acknowledgement ("if you know what I mean")
that a code is being used. Codes mean translations. And all of the above
needs to be put into another language besides that of transcription. It
will be a more subtle language than appears. For example, Nick has
already told us that Myrtle has no "features." He notices when he first
meets her that her face "contained no facet" (23) of beauty, which is a
direct way of describing mass without line. If features don't exist they
can't be modeled. They can, however, be invented by dialogue and con-
firmed by art. When Mrs. McKee says that Chester can "make something" of Myrtle's pose she acknowledges that Myrtle isn't much as is.
She needs some enabling fiction to become what she intends to be.

Calling on his muse means for McKee waving his hand in front of
his nose and becoming for the moment the incarnate form of artist and
shaman. Invoking whatever he has heard about lights and planes and
shadows, he represents perfectly art's falsification. If he provides image,
his wife and Myrtle provide text. The form of their dialogue has its own
conventions. The point is not that lies are exchanged but that they are
used to make up reality. That may well be the definition of salestalk—
and, if we reason by extension, of a great deal else.

Here are some possible interpretations or translations, which all
parties concerned know are contained within the dialogue. First, the
dress, which we know is pretentious and suspect may be a bit klunky—
it changes from "elaborate" to "adorable." That is a big change, in size
as well as style. There is a nice transformation within a transformation:

first, a woman changes, then she changes into something, then what she changes into changes by designation—but it isn't over yet. Although bought for an afternoon occasion among the Four Hundred the dress has been found hanging in the back of a closet off Broadway: a woman of resources will find any old thing to look good in. There is a lovely, complex lie in the phrase "when I don't care what I look like." There are five major lies in the sentence it comes from, and probably an unlimited amount of false inferences.

There are many possible translations for the code of salestalk, especially for a line like "if Chester could only get you in that pose I think he could make something of it." In fact, (although we have to remember that facts don't matter) Chester is incapable of making anything out of anything. And Myrtle is so far from being what her pose and dress represent that only film can gloss the difference. The great thing about the passage and that line is that everyone is lying, but no one is offended. Both women know that reality makes unfortunate but necessary demands upon illusion. Those in the dialogue must go along with these rules. And the rules stipulate here that Chester is an artist and his wife a critic; that Myrtle looks better after changing than before; and that she can be immortalized by a medium that doesn't have to listen to her. If Fitzgerald's test of intelligence is the ability to hold two contradictory ideas in mind at the same time, then it looks very much as if Myrtle has been underestimated. She understands the sequence of envisioning an identity from the instructions of media; linking it to her desire for change; working out the problem of appropriate style; finding an adequate but not necessarily truthful language; and finally of constructing herself through acquisition.

■

Like Gatsby, Myrtle Wilson has to make a transition, not between the yielding borders of adjacent class but between groups foreign to each other—and, in the twenties, hostile to each other. Myrtle is part of Labor but wants to become part of Capital. Gatsby wants to enter a closed social system, to penetrate the world of old money. The distance they must travel is inconceivable today or might be without documentation like that of Sheilah Graham (Fitzgerald's lover and author of *Be-*

loved Infidel) on her own social transformation. Graham, born Lily Shiel, learned to cross class boundaries in England during the early twenties. She lost her Cockney accent, learned how to dress, married a gentleman. The experience was embarrassing and painful—nothing like *Pygmalion*. She naturally enough learned to envy those above her and to despise herself. Her psychological crisis was delayed until she went to Hollywood in the early thirties as a columnist. Identified as a hostile critic of the studios she was systematically frozen out by the movie colony. This brought about a reversion in which she was convinced that her original identity had become as visible to others as it remained to herself. She had a recurrent depression: "Time and again when I attached myself to a group at someone's home and hopefully ventured a few words, the group seemed to dissolve and I would be left standing alone. Again the horror of rejection, of feeling *outside,* of being *scorned*— as if these people knew instinctively that I was of commoner clay— came over me. I took it, perhaps unconsciously, as an attack on my very right to exist." [23] It would be difficult to put things more clearly. Graham adds that she constantly feared "exposure," which is to say she feared Gatsby's fate. He and Myrtle determinedly hide their "original" selves. Graham hid "Shiel" in the hyperanglicized "Sheilah" in the same way that "Gatz" was contained but disguised in "Gatsby." The threat of "exposure" matters greatly to Gatsby and Graham and Myrtle Wilson— more than sexual guilt. At the Plaza Gatsby's pretensions collapse when Tom exposes his "real" identity. This is a problematic moment *because we expect to see something in the text of chapter 7 that isn't there, a defense by either Gatsby or Nick based upon the fairly transparent idea that we have the right to shape our own character. There should be something at this point, if only as a reminder that all money smells the same.* But once the exposure has been made, once appearance has been penetrated, the iron laws of social distinction apply. It is not only that Gatsby is a crook, or that Daisy is too weak to live with him knowing that—he is, in Sheilah Graham's phrase, "outside." The dilemma of the decade was that it promised two mutually contradictory things, change and acceptance.

Much advertising of the decade is addressed toward this dilemma. The brutal frankness of ads is now hard to believe, especially at a time when the consumer can do no wrong. Here is the *New Yorker* in 1926 on acceptability through acquired style: "The seeker after social popularity may be utterly without distinction in a dozen ways—in features, family, personality; she may even lack discretion. Yet social success may be hers!"[24] The life-changing commodity is a deodorant, *Odorono.* What now strikes the eye is not the product but the ideology: the ad is a defense of class boundaries and styles. It is written in an accessible code: to be without distinctive "features" (a phrase emphasized by both Nick and McKee, to our present puzzlement) is to fail a certain test. Commercial drawing of the twenties insists on facial linearity and regularity. "Features" are ovoid and very sharply sketched in ads or on *Post* covers. Virtually all drawings in ads, no matter what the product, show longheadedness.[25] Advertising seems to have taken its cue from anthropology and from the winning side of the immigration debate: no brachycephalics need apply. To be without "family" restates the proposition in a different way: it means race and religion as well as the intricate web of relationships as they are drawn in "Bernice Bobs Her Hair." The key phrase is "social popularity" or acceptance. Commercial art never tells us to be ourselves—it lectures us sternly about deficiencies of birth. Advertising prose is disciplinary. Men wear ties for golf and women must find a dress for each separate daily occasion. The ads of the twenties describe a world of right relationships. If there are dogs in an illustration, then there will be doormen to walk them. Where there are automobiles there are outfits to match them.[26] Most important, in pictures or in texts there are witnesses to tell us that passage from one social level to another needs approval. It may be that these ads tell us more directly than anything else about how everybody is doing everything.

Edmund Wilson speculated briefly about Fitzgerald's connection to these things in *Classics and Commercials.* Wilson thought that one of the most influential books of the twenties (it topped the Nonfiction Best Seller list for 1923) was *Etiquette* by Lillian Eichler—who had herself been transformed, into Emily Post. *Etiquette* (Wilson calls it an "extraordinary" book) has for him the powers of a novel by Galsworthy or Marquand. It shares the interests of Howells, he says, and of Henry James. Its preoccupation is the acquisition of a social identity—something that seems to demand not only education but duplicity. Ostensibly about manners at table and in the parlor, it is really about the ways in which people base their identities upon "models" of class and character. The social world it depicts is pyramidical; at the top are those who belong there, like the Oldnames and the Gildings; while below them, striving constantly to rise, are the rest of us. But there is something of a twist to what seems a familiar story: those aspiring to rise may not really deserve to do so. Emily Post's narrative is full of characters like the Unsuitables, Mr. Richan Vulgar, and the "pathetic Miss Nobackground" who cannot and probably should not rise. In the world as seen by Emily Post social activity consists of emulating those at the top and isolating those at the bottom of the pyramid.

Wilson believes that part of the reason for the book's popularity, and for any claim it may have to the fascinations of fiction, is its sense of social psychology. He states, "One feels, in fact, something like sadism in the whole approach of Mrs. Post. She likes to humiliate. She cannot tell us how charming Miss Wellborn is or how perfect is Mrs. Oldname's taste without putting in a little incident to show us this polish or grace making somebody else uncomfortable."[27] After acquaintance with the defenders of "civilization" in the early twenties we may recognize their logistic support; and see ulterior meanings in phrase, gesture, accent, and manner.

One remark of Wilson's in this essay should be pondered: "I was reminded, after reading *Etiquette,* of the late Scott Fitzgerald once telling me that he had looked into Emily Post and been inspired with the idea of a play in which all the motivations should consist of trying to do the right thing." That play might have been a comedy if it were confined to social tactics (there has not been an equal to their description since Thomas Hobbes: "By Manners, I mean not here, decency of behaviour; as how one should salute another, or how a man should wash his mouth, or pick his teeth before company, and such other points of the *small morals*").[28] But if Fitzgerald thought of Emily Post in anything like the way Edmund Wilson did then it was as a context for another purpose. The issue as Emily Post recognized it was the right to assume identity. At our end of the century that right has been conceded. In the early twenties it was opposed.

Only Yesterday, Frederick Lewis Allen's much-read informal history of the decade, has a very good account of other coercive fictions. Allen, like Edmund Wilson, is interested in narratives of social failure: "A wise man of the nineteen-twenties might have said that he cared not who made the laws of the country if he only might write its national advertising. For here were the sagas of the age, romances and tragedies depicting characters who became more familiar to the populace than those in any novel."[29] The subliterature of advertising was full of illustrations of social failure. There was the embarrassment of tooth decay and the banishment of those with B.O. There were the tears and shame and domestic woe of inept manners, and the cautionary tale of the girl who thought that filet mignon was a fish. "Be Free from All Embarrassment!" offered another work of Emily Post's, the *Book of Etiquette,* avoid halitosis said Listerine, and both really sold the same thing, escape from failure.

If you disliked what you were, you needed a new idea about truth. Gatsby aside, much else in his story depends on self-falsification. The theme was deep and wide in American culture during the twenties. And virtually all the major figures in *The Great Gatsby* are self-falsifying. They exist in a strange, dual relationship to themselves—sometimes, as in the case of Myrtle Wilson, actually living two lives. We see each character twice: as they would like to be seen, and as they are.

The omnipresent literature of middlebrow seriousness, magazines with admonitory columns, and advertisements and deep books with long words in them, offers continually to defend the original values of the old America—while it peddles things and styles that make for instant change. Few things seemed more interesting to Fitzgerald, evidently, than this contradiction. He was ideally situated to write a novel about the *difference* between act and idea, and act and feeling, which may be why Eliot wrote that *Gatsby* was "the first step that American fiction has taken since Henry James."[30] Eliot's "dissociated sensibility" was an idea of 1921.

Images also falsify. In Elizabeth Wilson's excellent study of modernity and fashion, *Adorned in Dreams,* we are reminded that photography, first praised for its realism, quickly changed the definition of fact. In movies, magazines, and newspapers—and especially in the depiction of fashion—"The great promise of photography was that it would tell the 'truth.' Yet the 'truth' of photography is only a more convincing illusion, selection and artifice lurking behind the seeming impartiality of the mechanical eye. Fashion drawings often give more accurate information."[31] Possibly we are to take literally the idea stated by Mrs. McKee that the camera can "make something" out of an old identity.

From changing "features" to furnishings: a *New Yorker* ad states the question that Myrtle seems to have asked herself: "How to make your apartment or house the most perfect background for yourself is your problem."[32] And a "problem" it is: the ad conveys advice to those who do not know how to be what they envision. It does not sell commodities directly but the ideas behind their use. The text promises consultation on "the principles for selecting your wall finishes, curtains, furniture and table appointments," and might have been designed for the second chapter of *The Great Gatsby*. It insists that "every room is a picture with yourself as the focal point." The idea is not so useful to fiction as the invention of Chester McKee, but it serves the same purpose of creating illusion through photographic fact. In the urban marketplace we create ourselves.

Novels like *The Great Gatsby* and *Old Goriot* are about the conflict between status and aspirations. No matter how convincing the chiffon dress or the Versailles tapestries or the Adam study, a change of identity does not go unchallenged. Gatsby and Myrtle acquire most of what they use to establish their sense of self. The story told about them is inevitably about their clothing; their houses or apartments; their food, drink, and even the sense of "art" appropriate to their new status. But the act of choice, of embodying a sense of self, creates problems greater than those of their original condition. They have been sold American ideas that turn out to be promissory, not negotiable. Myrtle and Gatsby do what all Americans are encouraged to do by the marketplace. It would appear that the falsification of their individual lives reflects a much larger falsification of ideas. Under the restless drive of industrial democracy we construct our own identities, but only within the limits of our theatrical abilities, and the limits imposed on us by our natural enemies, those who have arrived before us. Perhaps the best commentary on the idea of change comes from Balzac's *Cousin Bette,* a book that Fitzgerald addressed bitterly in 1925 when he began to realize the marketplace failure of *The Great Gatsby*. Balzac writes, "Have you ever noticed how, in childhood, or at the beginning of our social lives, we construct a model for ourselves, often quite unawares? A bank clerk, for instance, when he enters his manager's drawing room, dreams of possessing one just like it. If he makes his fortune twenty years later, it will not be the luxury then in fashion that he will introduce into his house, but the out-of-date luxury that fascinated him long ago. There is no end to the follies that issue from these retrospective envies, nor can we measure the effect of those secret rivalries that drive men to imitate the type that they have set themselves."[33] Gatsby and Myrtle seek a more modern "model" than that envisioned by Balzac, but it comes from the same place, those dreams "at the beginning of our social lives," which are satisfied only by possession, when things finally do become ideas.

Notes

1. Cited by Daniel Boorstin in *The Americans: The Democratic Experience* (New York: Random House, 1973), p. 113.

2. André Le Vot, *F. Scott Fitzgerald* (Garden City: Doubleday, 1983), p. 80. For contemporary surveys of daily life, see *Recent Social Trends in the United States: Report of the President's Research Committee on Social Trends* (New York: McGraw-Hill, 1933) and Robert S. Lynd and Helen Merrell Lynd, *Middletown* (New York: Harcourt Brace, 1929).

3. Paul T. Cherington, *The Consumer Looks At Advertising* (New York: Garland, 1985), pp. 42–43.

4. See for example the two-page spread for Paramount in the July 8, 1922, issue of the *Saturday Evening Post* (pp. 70–71). The thirty-five leading actors and actresses of Paramount studios are pictured in various states of intensely fashionable dress. For the actresses natural features are not enough: the ad emphasizes jewels, furs, hats, and the rest of *haute couture*. Head and shoulders only are depicted.

5. For a review of the modern argument on created demand, particularly of the work of John Kenneth Galbraith and of Herbert Marcuse, see Ronald Berman, *Advertising and Social Change* (Beverly Hills: Sage Publications, 1981), pp. 15–38.

6. See the editor's introduction to "May Day" and the first two pages of text in *The Short Stories of F. Scott Fitzgerald*, ed. Matthew J. Bruccoli (New York: Charles Scribner's Sons, 1989), pp. 97–98.

7. Christine Frederick, "Advertising Copy and the So-Called 'Average Woman,'" in *Masters of Advertising Copy*, ed. J. George Frederick (New York: Garland, 1985), p. 231.

8. William Wiser, *The Crazy Years: Paris in the Twenties* (New York: G. K. Hall, 1985), p. 160.

9. Elizabeth Wilson, *Adorned in Dreams: Fashion and Modernity* (Berkeley: University of California Press, 1985), p. 43. Here is Wilson's description of the modernist style of which Nancy Cunard was an archetype: "Chanel created the 'poor look,' the sweaters, jersey dresses and little suits that subverted the whole idea of fashion as display; although her trenchcoats and 'little nothing' black dresses might be made of the finest cashmere and her 'costume jewellery'—careless lumps of what looked like glass—were uncut emeralds and diamonds. Agile and full of movement, this was the spirit of modernity and futurism. As a style, it made a mockery of fashion; Cecil Beaton called it a nihilistic, anti-fashion look, and indeed it was one of the biggest contradictions of all to pay everything for a fashion that was invisible" (pp. 40–41).

10. Ibid., p. 62.

11. Ibid., p. 63.

12. According to *Middletown*, "Today the Middletown library offers 225 periodicals as against nineteen periodicals in 1890. Heavy, likewise, has been the increase of magazines coming into Middletown homes. Into the 9,200 homes of the city, there came in 1923, at a rough estimate, 20,000 copies of each issue of commercially published weekly and monthly periodicals" (p. 231). Cherington's 1928 assessment of consumption habits states that "the wide circulation of magazines and the motion picture theater have made common to even remote places the knowledge about new offerings in the consumer goods market" (p. 51).

13. Fernand Braudel, *The Structures of Everyday Life* (New York: Harper & Row, 1979), pp. 321–33.

14. This was clear to advertising from the beginning of the decade. See the maudlin and shrewd Charles Addison Parker, "Wanted—By the Dear Public," *Masters of Advertising Copy:* "And how often we advertising writers have fallen over this old stumbling block of a word 'Merchandise.' This package of rolled oats? . . . this is not merchandise, this is food for six hungry children. This player-piano? . . . this is something for a lonely man to lean his soul against and listen to the melodies she used to play" (p. 219). The best counter-intelligence for advertising remains Sinclair Lewis's *Main Street.* There is nothing like its mimicking of the smarmy tones and fake good-fellowship of copy text.

15. According to Christine Frederick in 1925 the following are universal characteristics of Everywoman in America: "lavishness on things decorative of herself," voluntary imitation of the "best people" and acceptance of "authority readily" (p. 233).

16. See Lewis Jacobs, *The Rise of the American Film* (New York: Harcourt Brace, 1939), p. 407. Shopgirl fantasies of the decade included *A Slave of Fash-*

ion, Ladies Must Dress, Pretty Clothes, Fashion Madness, Let's Be Fashionable, Charge It, and *Madame Peacock.* Ruth Prigozy's "From Griffith's Girls to Daddy's Girl: The Masks of Innocence in *Tender is the Night," Twentieth Century Literature* 26, no. 2 (Summer 1980): 189f. states that sexual and economic "confusion was mirrored and intensified by movies which, by the 1920s was unquestionably the most important new industry as well as entertainment medium in the country. It was also the most available showcase for consumer products, particularly cars, clothes, and home furnishings." And, "The twenties was still an era of female domination of films, because American values, whether expressed in dreams or nightmares, were still embodied in women" (p. 210).

17. Jacobs, *The Rise of the American Film,* p. 407. See the discussion of personal and industrial respectability in Hollywood in Neal Gabler, *An Empire of Their Own: How the Jews Invented Hollywood* (New York: Doubleday, 1988), pp. 104–44. "It was relatively simple to aestheticize oneself, to make oneself over" (p. 106). A theme in the lives of stars, directors, and producers became translated into the narratives of film. The enormous amount of success stories in the movies during the twenties was a mirror not only of national economic opportunity but of Hollywood's institutional frame of mind. However, see note 23 for the problems caused by opportunity both in and outside of films.

18. Fernand Braudel *The Structures of Everyday Life,* p. 323. For a discussion of wealth (rather than money, profit, or cost) in *The Great Gatsby,* see Michael Spindler, "The Rich Are Different: Scott Fitzgerald and the Leisure Class," in *American Literature and Social Change* (London: MacMillan, 1983), pp. 150f. See also the interpretation of fashion and commodities by Ross Posnock, "'A New World, Material Without Being Real': Fitzgerald's Critique of Capitalism in *The Great Gatsby,"* in *Critical Essays on F. Scott Fitzgerald's The Great Gatsby,* ed. Scott Donaldson (Boston: G. K. Hall, 1984), pp. 201f.

19. For the commercialization of Fitzgerald and his works, see Geof Cox, "Literary Pragmatics: A New Discipline. The Example of Fitzgerald's *Great Gatsby, Literature and History* 12, no. 1 (Spring 1986): 79f. See also Richard Anderson, "Gatsby's Long Shadow: Influence and Endurance," in *New Essays on The Great Gatsby,* ed. Matthew J. Bruccoli (Cambridge: Cambridge University Press, 1985), pp. 15f. According to Anderson,

> "Gatsby, and *The Great Gatsby,* again and again come to public attention in ways not necessarily dependent on having read the novel. They can be as ephemeral as advertisements and commercial exploitation. In 1964, for instance, an ad for the Plaza Hotel in New York, setting for the confrontation scene between Gatsby and Tom Buchanan, incorporated a passage from the novel. In 1968, the Eagle Shirt company marketed a Great Gatsby shirt, available in an appropriately rich array of hues, including West Egg Blue. In conjunction with the release in 1974 of the Paramount

film of *Gatsby,* there was a veritable flood of Gatsby products, ranging from phonograph recordings of 1920s music to Gatsby sportswear by McGregor, coiffures by Glemby Hair Salons, Teflon II Cookwear, and Ballentine's [sic] Whisky" (p. 23).

20. Phillips dominated covers of the *Saturday Evening Post* in 1922, although Rockwell had begun to make some contributions. The work of Phillips was much more "serious"—his brooding, pensive figures of women seem to have been intended to bring a touch of class to weekly entertainment: if the women on the covers he drew are a reflection of the audience they show that audience much more refined, better clothed and better looking than actuality. There is a good deal more content to both of these illustrators than appears: see for example the pioneering work of Wright Morris, *The Territory Ahead* (New York: Atheneum, 1963), pp. 113–29. A recent book by Milton R. Stern observes that "Rockwell's pictures are at once realistic, nostalgic, sentimental, and ideologically gratifying. In their intentions, effects, and audience, they are absolutely perfect products for the popular marketplace. They brilliantly exclude any examination of or question about the official ideologies upon which the American society is supposed to be based." From *Contexts For Hawthorne: The Marble Faun and the Politics of Openness and Closure in American Literature* (Urbana: University of Illinois Press, 1991), p. 83.

21. Alexis De Tocqueville, "In What Spirit the Americans Cultivate the Arts," in *Democracy in America,* ed. J. P. Mayer (Garden City: Doubleday, 1969), p. 467.

22. Cited by Daniel Boorstin in *The Americans: The Democratic Experience,* p. 444.

23. Sheilah Graham, *Beloved Infidel* (New York: Henry Holt, 1958), pp. 166–67. Gabler (*An Empire of Their Own*) argues on assimilation and *The Jazz Singer* (1927):

Jack's quandary is that he can bring Judaism to show business, but he cannot bring show business to Judaism—which to say that Judaism cannot be reinvigorated or revitalized in America or by America. It is alien to it. As Jack's mother says, "He has it [Jewish prayers] all in his head, but it is not in his heart," adding by way of explanation, "He is of America." In the end Jakie/Jack can affect no resolution. His father won't let him be an American; America won't let him be a Jew. Caught between the old life and the new, he is like the Hollywood Jews, of both and neither. In the play Jack yields to Jakie and replaces his father on Yom Kippur. Of course this surrender would never do for Jack Warner. In the film, Jack satisfies both masters. . . . He begs off opening night, and his Broadway premiere is postponed while he sings the 'Kol Nidre' in the synagogue. Then, in an epilogue, he brings down a packed house singing 'Mammy,' one of Jolson's trademarks, while out in the audience his own mama beams approval. How does Jack's (and the Jews') intractable problem suddenly get resolved? It is certainly not because Jack has found some way to navigate between these competing claims or because one has capitulated to the other, as Zukor and Mayer had surrendered their Judaism. The answer is that the movie, swiftly and painlessly, dissolves the problem altogether. Within the bounds of theatrical realism this could never happen, but the movies, after all, are a world of possibility where anything can happen" (p. 145).

Gabler's closing observation can be extrapolated: there would have been no evidence for self-change in the twenties if the movies had not shown it happening. Myrtle's dream of marriage and going out West with Tom is a movie ending that "dissolves the problem altogether" in more than one sense.

24. The *Odorono* ad appeared in the *New Yorker*, May 29, 1926, p. 47.

25. See the drawings of men and women in Earnest Elmo Calkins, *The Business of Advertising* (New York: Appleton, 1920), passim. Calkins was a patron saint of early advertising theory. Male and female illustrations compiled by him exaggerate "Nordic" or "Anglo-Saxon" features. His figures imitate British gentility in their "careless grace" (p. 304) and in the recollection of land-owner mannerisms. See the portfolio of ads of the twenties in the fiftieth anniversary issue of *Advertising Age: Twentieth Century Advertising and the Economy of Abundance* (April 1980), p. 85f. An H. J. Heinz ad portrays a deferential Hindu offering spices to a Heinz buyer in full *pukka sahib* outfit, complete to pith helmet.

26. Matching is an important conception. See the "Sports Ensemble by Régny: Car by Hupmobile" ad in *Advertising Age* above.

27. Edmund Wilson, "Books of Etiquette and Emily Post," in *Classics and Commercials* (New York: Noonday, 1950), pp. 381–82.

28. Thomas Hobbes, "Of the Difference of Manners," in *Leviathan,* ed. Michael Oakeshott (Oxford: Basil Blackwell, 1957), p. 63.

29. Frederick Lewis Allen, *Only Yesterday* (New York: Harper & Row, 1964), pp. 143–44. In "The Delegate From Great Neck," an imaginary dialogue, Edmund Wilson has Van Wyck Brooks address Fitzgerald on the confusion of fiction with advertising: "You are 'the man,' you told me, you know, at the beginning of our conversation, 'who has made America Younger-Generation-conscious.' Did you realize, when you used that expression, that you had dropped into the language of advertising?" There is then an interchange:

MR. FITZGERALD. I knew that what I said about making America Younger-Generation-conscious sounded like advertising. I was just making fun of the way that the advertising people talk.

MR. BROOKS. Let me remind you that Freud has shown us that the things we say in jest are as significant as the things we say in earnest—they may, in fact, be more significant, because they reveal the thoughts that are really at the back of our minds and that we do not care to avow to the world.

The Shores of Light (New York: Farrar, Straus and Young, 1952), pp. 151–52. Freud was (literally) in the air during the writing of *The Great Gatsby:* Franklin P. Adams did the lyrics and Brian Hooker, the music in 1925 for "Don't Tell Me What You Dreamed Last Night (For I've Been Reading Freud)." The ballad describes middle-class "conversation" about what "any psychoanalyst" would know. Reprinted in Sigmund Spaeth, *Read 'Em and Weep* (New York: Arco, 1959), pp. 226–27. The first edition of this collection was in 1926. But *The Beautiful and Damned* offers plentiful evidence that Fitzgerald was in Freud's audience.

30. Eliot's letter is reprinted in F. Scott Fitzgerald, *The Crack-Up,* Edward Wilson (New York: New Directions, 1945), p. 310.

31. Elizabeth Wilson, *Adorned in Dreams,* p. 158.

32. The *New Yorker,* December 5, 1925, p. 35.

33. Honoré De Balzac, *Cousin Bette,* (New York: Modern Library, 1958), p. 113. Balzac (like both Fitzgerald and Tocqueville) epitomizes social progress by reproductions made "without taste or skill" (p. 114). In an undated letter from Paris to Joseph Hergesheimer, probably May or June 1925, Fitzgerald wrote that the novel was selling badly and that it had been attacked by Burton Rascoe who would have misunderstood Balzac's *Cousin Bette* also. Matthew J. Bruccoli and Margaret M. Duggan, eds., *Correspondence of F. Scott Fitzgerald* (New York: Random House, 1980), pp. 166–67.

Seeing New York

■ *The Great Gatsby* alludes often to representational art that is old-fashioned no matter how new the medium. The resident spirit of photography, Chester McKee, prides himself on the correspondence between subject and title, and on his unalterable fidelity to location. He wants "to do more work on Long Island" (28) and, with that in mind, has objectified the scene in "Montauk Point—the Gulls" and "Montauk Point—the Sea." If you buy one of his pieces you will know where you are. Tom doesn't make art patronage easy, but he does have some "studies" (28) of his own in mind like "George B. Wilson at the Gasoline Pump." Myrtle has "scenes of ladies swinging in the gardens of Versailles" (25), which bring to interior decoration the literal image of social classiness. Nick may think of an El Greco but Daisy compares Gatsby to an advertisement. Jordan is "familiar" to the eye because she has been seen in "many rotogravure pictures" (18) while both Gatsby and his father carry around photographs whose claim is to make "real" what they image. His characters fit into the configuration of the early twenties, with its insistence on mass-produced actuality. We are comfortably in a world of photos and murals and portraits like the one in Mr. Carraway's office which validates resemblance. Much of the art we read about is designed to imitate, resemble, or represent. But the text sees things in different ways, and Fitzgerald only *seems* to have escaped modernism.

Visualization in the text is as divided as it is in the culture of the early twenties. The art of newspapers or photographs or tapestries or paintings described by Nick Carraway reflects one view—the regnant view—of artistic perception and its place in national life. Despite the advent of modernism there was such an understanding, and it might well be called official. It was expressed in great detail by the review of the past quarter-century in the report (1933) of the President's Research Committee on Social Trends. Few modernist concerns were addressed in this historical survey of pictorial art. It might be summarized as an attempt to think of pictorial art as a higher version, and a somewhat more sentimental version of photography.

In certain respects the report, a museum-piece, has to speak for itself, particularly in its attitude toward precision and quantification:

Not so long ago there was little to see in mural painting in America outside the Library of Congress and the Boston Public Library. Today there are admirable examples all over the country, nearly all of them directly attributable to the advertising value of a handsome bank or office building and department store. . . . Advertising men regard the year 1924 as significant, because it was then that *The Saturday Evening Post* adopted four-color work. Today the textile industry alone recognizes four hundred standard shades, of which, incidentally, more than one-third are used in women's stockings. This degree of differentiation is the more striking when we remember that in classical Latin only fifty words descriptive of color are to be found.[1]

Edmund Wilson satirized this mindset by listing nearly fifty of those aspiring colors, assuming unseriously that "The people who make women's hosiery must be employing poets."[2] There is not much in this report on national art about the Armory Show. There are, however, reflections on advertising and its "wholesome influence on our aesthetic standards."[3] The passage I have cited is clearly a majority statement. *The Great Gatsby* invokes majority responses to art, as in the Chester McKee episode, only to satirize them. But it works even more directly against the American grain. When Fitzgerald perceives and describes his landscape he uses techniques that never came from bourgeois realism. He was able to rely on readers' familiarity with new techniques of film and, to a certain extent, he could direct that attention to the poses, modeling, "scenes," and roles he describes. But, he also needed to describe in a new way. His dilemma is perhaps best stated by the remarkable contemporary "New Spirit" lecture of Apollinaire (1917): "In an epoch when the popular art *par excellence,* the cinema, is in essence a picture-book, it would be strange if poets did not try to create pictures for meditative, more sophisticated persons who find the productions of the film makers too crude."[4]

Fitzgerald's sense of place is charged with modernist sensibility. His description of "the city rising up across the river in white heaps and sugar lumps" (54) is abstract, monochrome, and cubist. His perspectives must seem to any audience, contemporary or not, as if they were interrupted by girders and columns, and formulated into sequences of lines and grids. The landscape of the novel is geometrical.

I'd like to compare two passages about Manhattan written at roughly the same time, the first from a piece by Rebecca West in the December 10, 1924, issue of the *New Republic* and the second from *The Great Gatsby*. The following West citation contains a passage about the same part of midtown described by Nick:

> I've been all over Manhattan Island, the oblong of mud and sand into which are driven the deep, deep foundations of New York. I've been down to the Assyrian quarter by the harbor. . . . I've been up to the Bronx, where along a road magniloquently called The [Grand] Concourse (magniloquently but not extravagantly, for it is in fact magnificent) apartment houses rise to incredible heights in what would be Roman grandeur were it not for the innumerable fire-escapes that mar them as projecting teeth mar even the handsomest women. I've walked for hours along Riverside Drive, which wanders for mile after mile on the steep edge of the island, past crazy Rhenish castles built in the good old days when the American millionaire had the courage of his convictions. . . . Fifth Avenue . . . becomes in its midmost and finest phase, a chasm between cliffs that rise up and up into the high inspired sunshine. At the base of the mountains of masonry walk crowds of people who are exhilarated as if they breathed high mountain air; for the atmosphere of New York, which is so full of electricity that you may give yourself a shock if you draw your hand along the brass rail of your bed, runs like wine in its people's veins.[5]

There is much about Madison, Lexington, and Park Avenues that recalls Nick's nighttime walks along them. But going across these streets is, according to West, "dull work walking among parallelograms." The intention of her description ("incredible," "innumerable," "crazy," "finest") is to tell you about the explicit connection between perceived things and feelings appropriate to them. Throughout the essay West sees midtown in representational detail and can register the difference between spire, gable, and dome. Most important is the universality of perception—she sees what you see and what both of you see has delimited meaning. It doesn't mean anything besides what it means. The world she describes needs no other perception because there isn't any more of it there. Nick Carraway's Fifth Avenue is somewhere else, in the City of Modernism, which the City of Man has become:

> I began to like New York, the racy, adventurous feel of it at night and the satisfaction that the constant flicker of men and women and machines gives to the restless eye. I liked to walk up Fifth Avenue and pick out romantic women from the crowd and imagine that in a few minutes I was going to enter into their lives, and no one would ever know or disapprove. Sometimes, in my mind, I followed them to their apartments on the corners of hidden streets, and they turned and smiled back at me before they faded through a door into warm darkness. . . .
>
> Again at eight o'clock, when the dark lanes of the Forties were five deep with throbbing taxi cabs bound for the theatre district, I felt a sinking in my heart. Forms leaned together in the taxis as they waited, and voices sang, and there was laughter from unheard jokes, and lighted cigarettes outlined unintelligible gestures inside. (46–47)

The passage is of historical as well as novelistic interest: part of modern times is modernism. It had taken fifteen years for the materials and techniques in it to become available. Cityscape may induce feeling, but that is not its primary reason for being. The importance of modernists, especially of Joyce and Eliot, "is that their pervasive assumption about the compellingly urban nature of the landscape in which we live, in which the city is . . . tends to localize the modern artist in the city, not because it is his modern material, but his modern point of view. Much modernist art has taken its stance from, gained its perspectives out of, a certain kind of distance, an exiled posture—a distance from local origins, class allegiances, the specific obligations and duties of those with an assigned role in a cohesive culture."[6] When Nick walks through the darkened streets of the city he is doing what the other minds of modernism habitually do, experiencing his apartness. It is almost a set piece of modernism: Joyce in Dublin, Hemingway in Paris, Eliot in London— Fitzgerald in a place where only geometry inheres. Nick's passage has no moral certainty: darkness and sexuality offer both a conscious and much deeper association, beyond editorial meddling. The mind is alone, and perception is not predetermined but rather caused by an unknown combination of conscious and unconscious drives.

This is the city of modernism, itself an interpretation of a state of mind. Some fragments out of which Eliot later constructed *The Waste Land* describe the unknown meaning of form in London streets in which we

> trace the cryptograms that may be curled
> Within these faint perceptions of the noise
> Of the movement, and the lights![7]

Nick's passage may have more specific comparative meaning. What he calls "the enchanted metropolitan twilight" is Eliot's "violet hour,"

> when the eyes and back
> Turn upward from the desk, when the human engine
> waits
> Like a taxi throbbing waiting.[8]

There is a larger resemblance when Eliot's "human engine" merges into the sameness of Fitzgerald's "men and women and machines." All are perceived objects with the same valencies when registered through "the constant flicker" of a reel of moving-picture film. In both writers the idea of organism takes on new definition. Nick hears modernism in the pulsation of engines that include the "sinking" or lowered heart. Hugh Kenner writes of Eliot's awareness that "the internal combustion engine altered people's perception of rhythm; little had been pervasively rhythmic earlier save one's own heart, one's lungs, the waves, and horses' hooves."[9] Elsewhere he writes that drills, valves, and exhausts become part of literary perception[10]—in *The Great Gatsby* we proceed by the movement of the "standard shift" within a universal geometry traced in air; observe human "straining" at a gas pump whose own rhythm never changes but which enforces the symbiosis of flow and hand; hear the noon whistle's reminder that Catullus was right. We even have "brakes" on our "desires" and there is an eternally ringing telephone that measures human relationship inversely by duration.

What Nick sees on Broadway is what Jake Barnes sees on the Avenue des Gobelins and what Alberto Giacometti saw—and did not see—on the Boulevard Montparnasse after his sudden realization that abstraction was more accurate than realism:

> It was as if I'd never seen it before, a complete transformation of reality, marvelous, totally strange, and the boulevard had the beauty of the *Arabian Nights*. Everything was different, space and objects and colors and the silence, because the sense of space generates silence, bathes objects in silence. From that day onward I realized that my vision of the world had been photographic, as it is for almost everybody, and that a photograph or film cannot truly convey reality, and especially the third dimension, space. I realized my vision of reality was poles apart from the supposed objectivity of a film.[11]

Apollinaire had stated that "productions of the film makers" were too unsophisticated to provide a new technology of art. His task, and that of Fitzgerald and Giacometti, was to describe perception in a way more real than realism. In the passage cited Nick perceives objects discontinuously, in the disorderly way that sight operates before its "view" is rationalized by the organizing mind. To go back to the Eliot fragment, the mind registers only "faint perceptions of the noise," that is, awareness before recognition, before the translation of noise into defined sound. Nick sees an abstract world because that is what the world looks like before it has been mentally rearranged. He relies on montage for the same reasons as modernist painters: there is no innate principle of composition in perception. He says that "men and women and machines" have the same visual values, which is true enough, but which is also a warning against moralizing. The scene is geometrical, made further so by the secondary realization that a grid is articulated by Fifth Avenue and those "lanes" of the numbered streets intersecting it. The geometry insistently recalled by the text, a matter of grids and patterns and intersections, will have much to do with Nick's narrative and our interpretation of its possibilities. One of the dominant conceptions of the passage is metabolism human and mechanical. By 1922, the "human engine" had entered discourse, and was now an indispensable idea. In some as yet not fully understood way the human and the mechanical, the romantic and the geometrical will have their own intersection.

There may be four hundred shades of stockings but there is only one color in Fitzgerald. The passage takes place in "warm darkness," which is more than a color and far less than a description. It is one of his many evasions of editorial censorship in the text, a compelling sexual image. Throughout the passage there is a powerful sense of sexual transference, with the penetration of hidden streets and openings in warm darkness; and throbbing engines waiting. Scenic perception is of no interest to the narration—what Fitzgerald has Nick see is the archetypal modernist subject, "Forms" in arrangement. The passage is about sensation and nearly every sense is affected: there is a "feel" of the city; then the flickering view past the "restless eye"; the sensation of warmth; and again feeling the noise of the engines replicated by pumping of the heart. The disposition—"Forms leaned together"—is abstract and economical enough to challenge minimalism. We become conscious not only of Fitzgerald's descriptive reluctance but of his concentration on certain kinds of modes and objects.

■

Stanley Sultan has warned us that influence and relationship must be argued: there can be no point in simply stating that all sources of a work are influences on it.[12] Nor can there be a simply "temporal" idea about source and influence because not everything produced at the same historical moment is related. I will, accordingly, qualify any statements I make on where Fitzgerald got ideas about ideas. One link to modernisn was Edmund Wilson, who early admired and analyzed the mass culture of Broadway. Both he and Fitzgerald were intensely sympathetic to the vitality of Broadway—and to its vulgarity, which neither sidestepped. Both depicted Broadway lyrics, ads, marquees, talk, and salesmanship —and entertainment itself was one of the great subjects of modernism. But this was part of a wider movement that early realized that the commonplace and commercial were artistically interesting. The realization cut both ways: The July 1922 issue of *Vanity Fair* situates Mary Pickford's incredibly elaborate De lage across the page from a photo of a thoughtful James Joyce, a few pages after Tristan Tzara's "Some Memoirs of Dadaism." Style was a commodity and modernism was a style fit for entertainment.

If only descriptively, I want to establish two points about the text of *The Great Gatsby:* it is intensely sympathetic to the objectified world of mass culture; and it treats that world in a style conforming to modernism. The location is the city and reality is urban. In dealing with Conrad (both source and influence for Fitzgerald), Stanley Sultan writes that "the impress of urban industrial civilization on the human spirit, central to 'Prufrock,' is equally central to 'Heart of Darkness.' "[13] But any interpretation of Fitzgerald is bound to be different, because it must take the idea of the "industrial" in a different sense. Hugh Kenner reminds us in *A Homemade World* about the difference in literary attitude toward cityscape as modern literature began to be shaped. Henry James saw "a welter of objects and sounds in which relief, detachment, dignity, meaning, perished utterly and lost all rights." But Ezra Pound saw the city as Fitzgerald would, in terms of a different kind or order: "lighted windows. Squares after squares."[14] Pound was conscious of engineered, replicated order.

The most formidable recent interpretation of modernist "language" and "vision," Marjorie Perloff's *The Futurist Moment,* establishes intersections between language and image, between one version of modernism and another. On collage, she argues against the theory of Jameson about the hostility of art to industrialism: "the great Cubist and Futurist artists—Picasso, Braque, Gris, Boccioni, Severini, Carrà, Malevich, Tatlin—were quick to accept 'the world of commodity production and of the mass media' as a challenge rather than a threat, a new source of imagery and of structuration."[15] It is clearly the superior argument: for Boccioni "bodies and objects" are both like "bits of machinery"; the title of Juan Gris's *Banjo and Glasses* indicates that it is about two produced objects, while the picture itself is full of the angles and lines of straight-edge manufacturing; Carrà said that "*ordinary things* are the only real links we have between the essence of the world and ourselves."[16] Picabia paints levers and armatures; De Chirico, blueprints; Mondrian, the *Broadway Boogie-Woogie* that looks on canvas like Nick Carraway's New York, all line, movement, and color. From manufacturing to painting, and from painting everywhere else, as in the work of Picasso: "Within a few years, collage and its cognates—montage, construction, assemblage —were playing a central role in the verbal as well as the visual arts."[17]

"Modern Narrative," in Frederick Karl's argument, is a matter of Conrad, to be sure—but also of Picasso. Technically considered it is full of "space, light, color" treated in special ways.[18] Karl notes in his discussion of narrative cubism's "perception"; and Mondrian's fascination with "lines, horrizontals, verticals, and diagonals" that make up his "grid style."[19] Both Perloff and Karl are convinced of the connection between image and print, and of the silent communication between the arts. There are two points common to both critics that ought to be emphasized here: (1) Karl states that modernism began with "defiance of the traditional sense that only fine materials should be used";[20] (2) Perloff maintains that even a movement like futurism, low in the hierarchy of arts, resulted nevertheless in the revisualization of "art or music, theater or film."[21] The ordinary—especially billboards, cars, and signs— became part of narrative. These things, which fascinated futurism, ended by capturing the attention of "higher" forms of art—and of advertising, which is to say they became part of a mutual vocabulary of image.

A novel so extensively referential to photography—itself on the low end of critical valence—becomes necessarily connected to objects, masses, and lines. And also to the concept that a photograph can be taken of anything. "Big" scenes will not only be photographically conscious but will include things like "a plate of cold fried chicken" and two bottles of ale. To establish the hospitality of modernism to inclusion, it is useful to go to Eliot and Pound, but it is also useful to go down the scale. Here is Susan Sontag's account of "marginal beauty" and value:

> In principle, photography executes the Surrealist mandate to adopt an uncompromisingly egalitarian attitude toward subject matter. (Everything is "real.") In fact, it has—like mainstream Surrealist taste itself—evinced an inveterate fondness for trash, eyesores, rejects, peeling surfaces, odd stuff, kitsch. Thus, Atget specialized in the marginal beauties of jerry-built wheeled vehicles, gaudy or fantastic window displays, the raffish art of shop signs and carousels, ornate porticoes, curious door knockers and wrought-iron grilles, stucco ornaments on the façades of run-down houses. . . .

Bleak factory buildings and billboard-cluttered avenues look as beautiful, through the camera's eye, as churches and pastoral landscapes. More beautiful, by modern taste.[22]

Sontag reminds us that this attitude was not born in the lower critical latitudes: it was Baudelaire who identified poetry with the pursuit of "objects" produced by "the goddess of Industry." There is a direct line to Eliot—but of Eliot's concern with these things Hugh Kenner has already drawn up a catalog in *The Mechanic Muse*. There is another point raised by Susan Sontag, that abstractions and "machine forms" came to dominate the photographic imagination—and the world of printed image—from 1920 to 1935.[23] "By the 1920s," she states, "Readers of the popular press" were invited to believe in Futurist and Surrealist ideas like "the beauty of machines."[24] Fitzgerald's notebooks include the reiteration of geometrical and mechanical form as part of a plenum of actuality:

SEEN IN A JUNK YARD

Dogs, chickens with few claws, brass fittings, T's elbow, rust everywhere, bales of metal 1800 lbs., plumbing fixtures, bathtubs, sinks, water pumps, wheels, Fordson tractor, Acetylene lamps for tractors, sewing machine, bell on dingy, box of bolts, No. 1 van, stove, auto stuff (No. 2), army trucks, cast iron, body hot dog stand, dinky engines, sprockets like watch parts, hinge all taken apart on building side, motorcycle radiators, George on the high army truck.[25]

The Great Gatsby is about image and print from "the popular press" in more than one way. Among its silent characters are the swarm of "photographers and newspaper men in and out of Gatsby's front door" (127). Among the effects of commercial image and print is the text of the novel: " 'You resemble the advertisement of the man,' she went on innocently. 'You know the advertisement of the man——' " (93). But chief, I think, of the effects of what Sontag defines as a new aesthetic, or at least the opening of a new field for perception was the matter of urban form.

Throughout the text Fitzgerald's perceptions are defined by light, line, and movement—"Over the great bridge, with the sunlight through

the girders making a constant flicker upon the moving cars" (54)—
which counteract the instructions of realism. Mechanism is an insistent
part of Fitzgerald's perception. It is not merely that Daisy's voice is
"artificial" or that Catherine Wilson's face is out of "alignment" or that
Tom's body is described in terms of its "leverage." The context, cityscape, is shaped by skyline, train tracks, roads, columns, girders, and
rows of windows in even larger rows of buildings that extend their shape
and replicate their form. Fitzgerald does not find it dull work among
parallelograms.

The intense geometry of description in the text reflects the inter-
communication of the arts. There was "a modern art from Chaplin to
dancer Josephine Baker, from movie theater to the poster."[26] That much
according to art theory; believable when we go to the first-hand evidence. In his 1924 essay on "The Machine Aesthetic," Fernand Léger
assumes that "the power of geometric form" in manufactured objects
(in this case airframes at the Aviation Show of the Paris Fair) makes
these objects completely characteristic of art.[27] Pounds's *Patria Mia* of
1913 emphasizes "high windows . . . lighted windows. . . . Squares after
squares of flame."[28] And, in commenting on Pound's linkage of subject
to form, Perloff states that his city needs a certain kind of expression:
"prose may well be superior to poetry because prose can be related to
the American instinct for 'action and profit.' In particular, he cites 'the
composition of advertisements' as a 'symptomatic prose' in which 'there
is some attention paid to a living and effective style.' The next step was
to carry such 'symptomatic prose,' the language of advertisements, over
into the realm of art."[29] We may suspect a particular kind of language,
that of the poster, which combines text and image. And the enormous
simplicity of Fitzgerald's cityscape, its concentration on a few salient
images and the distance we are from its horizon suggests very strongly
the new modernist field of poster art.

The exceptional collection by Dawn Ades in her book *The 20th-
Century Poster: Design of the Avant Garde* has a great deal of evidence not
only about the character of "symptomatic prose" in the twenties but
also about its motifs.[30] Posters of the period were often of violently geometrical design; color was simple; both natural and artificial light was
exceptionally clear and strong; prominent were manufactured objects;

throughout were grid patterns of tracks and reiterated rows of windows in tall buildings. Poster art was not only about urban found objects but about endless repetition, especially of the structure and appearance of buildings—squares after squares. Posters made the twenties audience familiar to a certain extent with the mixture of forms—and certainly with the omnipresence of texts. They are, if not the most abstract of modernist forms, at least the most compressed.

Fitzgerald seems to have responded to these pictorial values. The Cugat illustration for the first edition cover that he wanted so badly is itself a poster, with its skyline intensely colored but in one dimension. The background (which takes up nearly all the space in the illustration) is a single block of blue. Its sketch of a female face over the skyline is a kind of visual shorthand. Not only the subject of the Cugat illustration mattered for the first readers of the novel but also its form and disposition. There is no attempt to display proportion, and visual perspective bears no relationship to older expectations. Like the text, the cover illustration is sure only of its geometry.

Perception in *The Great Gatsby* is modernist and reductive. Nick and the reader will see a shadow moving westward "down the white chasms of lower New York" (46), but that is all we will see. We ought to think for a moment about the monochrome rectangles of the skyline seen from the Queensboro Bridge or from the drive in Central Park, or (it is the total of description) the red-belted waterlines of ocean-going ships. What we "see" in Fitzgerald's cityscape is linear form or circular form like gas pumps in primal red within reiterated circles of pools of yellow light. Form and color are primal, and have little to do with conventional pictorial sensibility. We often see its poster terminology: large blank surfaces; little detail or brushwork (surfaces are unbelievably and unrealistically smooth); bloc coloration (at one point, in describing the skyline Fitzgerald uses the word "block" to describe light). There is the intense focus of poster perception—Fitzgerald does not use perspective in his cityscape descriptions, nearly all of which are flat. The world Nick sees is geometric (plane geometry, without depth) and has an order of its own. It has mathematical beauty and of course is suffused with the relationships of line, angle, and square. But in a world so largely dominated by geometry there may not be verities of other kinds. It may be too much to expect the reification of moralities. I cannot emphasize too much the role that objectified reality plays in this novel, because it clearly sets limits to expectations. The order of things, being bound by their geometry, is bound also by the principles of that geometry. Dreams are bounded by rules.

Fitzgerald establishes his human subjects through what Meyer Schapiro calls "the intrinsic powers of colors and lines, rather than through the imaging of facial expressions":[31] "The sister, Catherine, was a slender, worldly girl of about thirty, with a solid sticky bob of red hair and a complexion powdered milky white. Her eyebrows had been plucked and then drawn on again at a more rakish angle but the efforts of nature toward the restoration of the old alignment gave a blurred air to her face" (26). The first thing we "see" (although, for the second time in this chapter, Fitzgerald has used the term "blurred" to qualify perception) is the conflict of art and nature. It will be given new definition. There is art within art, the commentary of prose on what turns out to be painting. Catherine Wilson is entirely frontal and described only as an economical "solid" or primal patch of red over another of white. The view is entirely flat and makes no effort at reproducing three-dimensional reality. There are only "lines and masses."[32] Catherine is a stick figure surmounted by two circles on one of which linearity is repeated and patterned through "alignment" and "angle." This is a modernist painting, done by the subject. There is the same amount and kind of facial detail as in Picasso's *Girl With a Mandolin* (1910) and considerably less than in Modigliani's *Seated Woman* (1918).[33] The connection of techniques was important to writing: Eliot's "avoidance of three-dimensional portrayals in characterisation recalls the voluntary falsifications of perspective and spatial relationships, or the intentional suppressions of detail, in modern painting."[34] There are no eyes—but when eyes are needed, Fitzgerald knows how to provide them.

Tom Buchanan's "shining, arrogant eyes" (9) have a cubist relationship to his face, mouth, and (intentionally a play on ideas, I think) to the unfilled or blank space of his head. One of the working principles of cubism is that "appearance" is understood to be only the manifestation of what is "internal."[35] The concept is as old as literature, but like much in modernism it was made new. Shortly before Fitzgerald began dealing with the eyes of Tom Buchanan and those of Dr. Eckleburg, Yeats wrote the following:

> great eyes without thought
> Under the shadow of stupid straw-pale
> locks. . . .[36]

This is the spirit of the age in "Nineteen Hundred and Nineteen" (both supernatural and metaphorical). The poem appeared originally in the *Dial* under a title that flatly stated its meaning: "Thoughts upon the Present State of the World." Modernist techniques are associative even at their most compacted. The "dominance" of Tom's eyes over the rest of his face suggests, as in Yeats, more politics than physiology.

There seem not to be any eyes in Wolfshiem's face at first: "A small flat-nosed Jew raised his large head and regarded me with two fine growths of hair which luxuriated in either nostril" (55). Eventually eyes and mouth attain form, but Wolfshiem's "expressive" (expressionist?) nose seems to replace their functioning. Expressive noses are a trademark of Picasso. The nose will take the domain and function of the head itself, become a surrogate head in which the hairy nostrils look like eyes.[37] Myrtle seen for the first time looks like a Cycladic torso and her dress is far more detailed than her face. Seen for the last time she is a mechanism that (to use Nick's phrase) has been "smashed up." Myrtle's death is understood through a language (and through the laws) of mechanism: different narrators recall the swerve of the automobile, reaching for the wheel, feeling the shock of collision. Her death and Gatsby's are perceived and described through morally neutral form. The curvature of Myrtle's "form," her body kneeling on the road and Gatsby's body circling in the current are self-expressive. Fitzgerald does not explain what he sees because what he sees may contain all the meaning that he sees.

It would be difficult to find critics better able to explain abstract painting and poetry than E. H. Gombrich, Meyer Schapiro, and Hugh Kenner —all of whom have analyzed the rendition of surface and character in early modernism. Fitzgerald's variations may perhaps be accounted for by Gombrich's essay "On Physiognomic Perception." Historians and others who need explicit interpretation have, according to Gombrich, "compulsions" to "make sense of the unintelligible." But artists have a different sense of the "unintelligible." Certainly Fitzgerald does. He often invokes the idea (the phrase and its equivalents) but only to admit its constraints. A tremendous amount of perception—not description, but the act of sensory perception—in *The Great Gatsby* is by admission of its narrator imperfect and even unavailing. This goes against the grain of intellectuals who, according to Gombrich, demand that all things "have a physiognomy, some kind of expressive character." The historian's mentality guarantees error because it imposes meaning. The artist sees without "distinctions" so that what is seen may well be the simple existential facts of "accidental shapes and random movements."[38] The artist, like the child, may see no differentiation "between the inanimate and the animate, let alone between things and symbols." That picture we get of Wolfsheim is not, to use a word invoked by Gombrich, "diagrammatic." It tells us how Fitzgerald perceives things rather than what Wolfshiem is like. Fitzgerald consistently has Nick Carraway see things in terms of "imaginary geometries."[39] Nick describes place, character, and appearance in terms of lines, circles, mass, and color.

In *A Sinking Island,* Hugh Kenner writes that "Machinery confronted you in London everywhere you looked," accounting for the factual details of Eliot's landscape. There was a new sense of geometry formulated by macadam strips, underground "Tubes" and the omnipresent "webs of water-pipes, sewer-pipes, gas-pipes." Modernist urban geometry came to literature through paintings "that leaped like lightning from country to country, Paris-Moscow-Munich-London, unchecked by Babel's barriers. And by 1913 designs rectilinear as a city grid, busy and cacophonous as Oxford Circus, brought the unwanted news that Constable's England and Jane Austen's was gone forever."[40] Within ten years of that date Fitzgerald and Hemingway saw such patterns as aesthetic norms. Their descriptions of New York and Paris perceive linearity, patterned color and especially *artificial* light. Urban scenes not only objectify culture as artifice—landscape may be alienated, suggestive of character and feeling. It states what we may not. A passage like the following from *The Great Gatsby* insists on geometric form modifying and containing a strongly romantic moment:

I wanted to get out and walk eastward toward the park through the soft twilight but each time I tried to go I became entangled in some wild strident argument which pulled me back, as if with ropes, into my chair. Yet high over the city our line of yellow windows must have contributed their share of human secrecy to the casual watcher in the darkening streets. (30)

There are lines and squares within lines and squares: the rectangles of the Park, the apartment and its rooms, the blocks formed by streets. The ropes are lines and the entangling net a system of linear stress. It is important to realize that the "mass cultural forms" of skyscrapers were "metonyms for the modern."[41] To see them is to make a connection between values, and to *state* them textually, as Fitzgerald does, is to draw another kind of connection, to announce modernism. And, of course, to make some contingent recognitions: the "line" of windows is a progression of forms with implication; to live in a world so mathematically organized and replicated is to sense the limits of will. Whatever the promises of life may be they cannot exceed its laws.

The story that follows, of Tom's seduction of Myrtle, combines body and object in striking ways. Suddenly and lyrically, Myrtle's "warm breath poured over me" (30), Nick says, as Myrtle begins to find a language for her experience. Virtually everything in that language, from things remembered to sensations experienced, has some connection to industrial fact. Myrtle seems unwilling or unable to tell us what Tom looked like or how she felt. She says first that there were those "two little seats facing each other that are always the last ones left on the train" (31). The affair begins in that angled space moving on tracks. Tom looks like an illustration and her view goes from him to the advertisements overhead. She can remember or wants to discuss only his dress suit and patent leather shoes and "white shirt front pressed against my arm" (31). When she says, "I was so excited that . . ." we expect the conclusion to be sexually revealing. But the rest of the sentence is, "when I got into a taxi with him I didn't hardly know I wasn't getting into a subway train." The difference between Nick's description of Myrtle and Myrtle's description of falling in love is meant, I think, to suggest more than her intellectual limits. She is part of what she imagines and remembers, a world of objects.

Much of what we read or "see" in *The Great Gatsby* is assumed to be factual. It establishes, or should establish, common identity or appearance as more than one mind perceives it. But we cannot rely on that—what, for example, is the reader to do with the line about Daisy, "A damp streak of hair lay like a dash of blue paint across her cheek"? (67). There are ways of interpreting yellow music and blue gardens but they probably don't include natural appearance under altered conditions. It would be a waste of time to argue that under a certain light hair looks blue. Eventually we would have to conclude that Fitzgerald is a kind of superior photographer who knows that at certain times of day grass seems blue, or that yellow is a convenient symbol for gold. But I think the phrase about Daisy concerns "the self-sufficiency of forms and colors."[42] The critical problem is not that he alters facts but that he describes perceptions.

One of Fitzgerald's most important stylistic techniques is the replacement of description by perception. Given that this novel is often romantic and lyrical, we expect it also to be intensely evocative. But it is often denuded of description, focused not affectively but on line, mass, space, and motion. It deals with color, as in the brief description of Daisy's hair, as a possibility rather than as a characteristic.

When Nick and Gatsby go for the first time to New York, the landscape (and those in it) is constituted by verticals and horizontals in black and white. There is one exception, the extremely condensed "glimpse of red-belted ocean-going ships" (54). The car moves along straight roads and geometrical forms, past ships defined only by line and along streets squared almost infinitely by their "cobbled" components. The triangular valley "opened out on both sides" and along plotted curves the car "twisted among the pillars of the elevated." We see sunlight only "through the girders" of the bridge and through that same cinematic "flicker" imaging men and women and machines near Broadway. Things organic are expressionist: those "tragic eyes and short upper lips" and "yolks of . . . eyeballs" (55) are themselves manifestations of geometry; lines and circles, self-sufficient forms. There are many ignored opportunities for description, like that "hearse heaped with blooms." It is important to realize how often Fitzgerald chooses to be minimalist in his evocations.

Space disorients. Different kinds of light cause the perception not of the object viewed but of intervening girders, pillars, angles and "thin elongating glints upon the roadside wires" (64). A passage like the following seems prose Chagall: "We passed a barrier of dark trees, and then the façade of Fifty-ninth Street, a block of delicate pale light, beamed down into the Park. Unlike Gatsby and Tom Buchanan I had no girl whose disembodied face floated along the dark cornices and blinding signs and so I drew up the girl beside me, tightening my arms. Her wan, scornful mouth smiled, and so I drew her up again closer, this time to my face" (63). The horizon is met first by trees, then by the broken rectangles of skyline. Language is part of geometric perception: light occurs in the form of a "block" and darkness is sensed by its effects on the angular "cornices." One kind of light is pale, diffused from a distance through a sequence of window frames, necessarily changing intensity. The other kind of light is harsh and even "blinding," forcing us to realize again how difficult it is in this text to see anything clearly. The second kind of light interested Hemingway who described it repeatedly in the Paris chapters of *The Sun Also Rises* as the light of "electric signs." In both novels it corresponds to the sexual energies and demands that it illuminates.

Fitzgerald described this scene or part of it twice, the first time in the 1925 edition of *The Great Gatsby,* and then once more in his 1932 autobiographical essay, "My Lost City." The second time recalls the first with precision: "riding south through Central Park at dark toward where the façade of 59th Street thrusts its lights through the trees."[43] There are specific terms common to both recollections. The later passage leads into a vision of the "mystery and promise" of New York that echoes passages of the novel. New York was "lost" to Fitzgerald for a number of reasons, chief among them his alcoholism, which he says prevented his functioning as a writer. But this particular patch of midtown has other associations. The night imagery of New York is connected to dreams, and to the *ur*-dream of the text, the memory of Eden. Something else is brought out with great clarity, the evanescent light and gathering dark are evidence of impermanence. Fitzgerald sees things that happen only once, as they are experienced. After that they belong only to dreams.

According to Meyer Schapiro, "gestures and bodily movements . . . are also forms."[44] It may be that Hemingway's respect for and envy of Fitzgerald proceed from his ability to describe movement with modernist economy. Fitzgerald works close to the bull, as when he describes the way that Tom Buchanan holds or hits people. There are passages in *The Great Gatsby* not likely to attract notice but whose concision— "The sharp jut of a wall" (44)—works to reduce description but enlarge perception; in this case to provide for the narrative underlying angularity and geometric insistence. Action takes place against the resistance of rules, laws, and material facts. There is a subterranean sense of the factuality of life that finally defines the impossibilities of dreams. The sensory and quantifiable delineation of the material world ("the bright door sent ten square feet of light volleying out. . . . The pebbles of the drive crunched under his feet" [71–72]) describes its limits. But the felt presence of geometry in the text is counterpoised. It is not always possible to see things in definition.

There is another kind of language of description:

> Through all he said, even through his appalling sentimentality, I was reminded of something—an elusive rhythm, a fragment of lost words, that I had heard somewhere a long time ago. For a moment a phrase tried to take shape in my mouth and my lips parted like a dumb man's, as though there was more struggling upon them than a wisp of startled air. But they made no sound and what I had almost remembered was uncommunicable forever. (87)

There is much in *The Great Gatsby* that resists description. Nick will tell us that he sees only "Forms" or that certain gestures are "unintelligible" or that memory is "uncommunicable." Important passages are devoted to informing us that vision is "blurred" or that accurate perception is impossible:

> the ash-grey men swarm up with leaden spades and stir up an impenetrable cloud which screens their obscure operations from

your sight (21). . . . looking with blind eyes through the smoke (31). . . . I can still read the grey names and they will give you a better impression than my generalities (49). . . . looking at him with unfathomable delight (61). . . . unreal (64). . . . inconceivable (72). . . . indefinite (73). . . . nebulous (74). . . . ineffable (77). . . . It is invariably saddening to look through new eyes at things upon which you have expended your own powers of adjustment (81). . . . Incalculable (85). . . . mysterious (86). . . . elusive (87) . . . . indefinable (94). . . . The prolonged and tumultuous argument that ended by herding us into that room eludes me (98). . . . it was all going by too fast now for his blurred eyes (119). . . . incoherent (122). . . . unfamiliar (126). . . . a faint, barely perceptible movement (126).

Narration is overwhelmingly concerned with the difficulties and impossibilities of describing experience or "moulding its senselessness into forms" (92). Elusive description characterizes the narrator, but also implies the resistance of art to conventional technique. The book is full of words like "form" and "impression" and "perception" that do not have single meanings. In its ending the phrase "incoherent failure" (140) forces our attention not only on scene but also narration.

Fitzgerald will use the word "grotesque" (137) to apply to distorted perception. He will at frequent intervals qualify the power of visual—or intellectual—resolution. In no respect is he more modernist than this reluctance to define. The numerous introductions into the text of qualified and distorted perception suggest that reality is too complex to be known by realism; and that relationships are too relative to be known. The actual, to rephrase philosophy, may also be unknowable. We cannot fully "see" things in terms of their forms—and we may not be able to see them in terms of their other meanings.

One of the most revealing passages in the text of *The Great Gatsby* states the more than physical disappearance of Daisy Buchanan. The dialogue describing this sounds as if it were written by Beckett:

"Left no address?"
"No."
"Say when they'd be back?"

"No."

"Any idea where they are? How I could reach them?"

"I don't know. Can't say." (128)

This too is a distortion, a reminder by the text of a larger discorrelation. The absence of any meaningful language is appropriate. It is an empty space in the story. On the other hand, all that is meaningful in the connection between Nick, Daisy, and Gatsby may have been stated.

One of the best recent essays on *The Great Gatsby* concentrates on perception in the text: the novel is written in "a composite style whose chief demonstrable point appears to be the inadequacy of any single style (or single means of perception, point of view) by which to do justice to the story." Beneath the surface, "*Gatsby* is boiling with conflict—chiefly the conflict of new and old, the inadequacy of the old ways and means to deal with the new world of the twentieth century. Thus, behind its seemingly bland and polite surface, *Gatsby* is, in many ways, a wildly experimental novel."[45] Important parts of the text are in the conditional and interrogative modes. Description of act, and expecially intention, and even experience is often accompanied by disclaimers about accuracy. Observation is compromised by misperception. Important terms—like "perception" itself—or "impression" and its many equivalents annul the claims of realism. But the issue is not realism itself, but rather positivism. Is it likely that we will get the delineation or definition of Daisy by line and mass even when she says that Pammy's "got my hair and shape of the face" (91). Everything is not only uncertain but relative. Is that because Nick is not very good at noticing things? Or because he cannot do justice to Daisy? Or is it rather because Fitzgerald no longer believes in positivism, which is, as a good dictionary states, the belief that "knowledge is based on natural phenomena and their spatiotemporal properties and invariant relations"?[46] As for spatiotemporal properties, we ought to try this on for size:

He told me all this very much later, but I've put it down here with the idea of exploding those first wild rumors about his antecedents, which weren't even faintly true. Moreover he told it to me at a time of confusion, when I had reached the point of believing everything and nothing about him. So I take advantage of this short halt, while Gatsby, so to speak, caught his breath, to clear this set of misconceptions away. (79)

The language of confusion and false belief applies to the narration as well as to—even more than to—the point at issue. The passage ranges from the facts of Gatsby's life to their eventual acknowledgment before the time of setting them down but after their misconception. Which is, in turn, before the confusion engulfing not only the narrative moment but also the narration. It is unlikely that a single reading can establish the chronology of these three sentences. Realism is built on positivism; modernism is built on relativity. Indefiniteness, hopeless complication, and the failure of objectivity are characteristics as well as circumstances. The ambiguity of time, space, and form in the text is a technique for stating the nature of all relationship.

Notes

1. *Recent Social Trends in the United States: Report of the President's Research Committee on Social Trends* (New York: McGraw-Hill, 1933), pp. 979–80.

2. Edmund Wilson, "Current Fashions," in *The American Earthquake* (New York: Farrar Straus Giroux, 1958), p. 76.

3. *Recent Social Trends*, p. 978. The long essay on "The Arts in Social Life" acknowledges "Modernism" but its heart is in Zenith and Gopher Prairie: by far the most involved discussion takes place in categories like "Art and Business." There is a corrective in Walter Pach's contribution on "Art" in *Civilization in the United States*, ed. Harold E. Stearns (London: Jonathan Cape, 1922), pp. 227–41. Pach argues that the Armory Show of 1913 did in fact have a public effect and by 1922 important Modernist collections had begun to be formed. He thought that "The steel bridges, the steel buildings, the newly designed machines, and utensils of all kinds we are bringing forth show an adaptation in function that is recognized as one of the great elements of art" (p. 241).

4. Guillaume Apollinaire's "The New Spirit and the Poets" is reprinted in Francis Steegmuller's *Apollinaire: Poet Among the Painters* (New York: Penguin, 1986), pp. 278–89.

5. Rebecca West, "Impressions of America," *New Republic*, December 10, 1924, p. 65–66.

6. Malcolm Bradbury, "The Cities of Modernism," in *Modernism 1890–1930*, ed. Bradbury and James McFarlane (Harmondsworth: Penguin, 1983), p. 100.

7. Cited by Ronald Bush, *T. S. Eliot: A Study in Character and Style* (New York: Oxford University Press, 1984), p. 56.

8. T. S. Eliot, "The Waste Land," in *Collected Poems 1909–1962* (New York: Harcourt, Brace & World, 1970), p. 61.

9. Hugh Kenner, *The Mechanic Muse* (New York: Oxford University Press, 1987), p. 9.

10. Hugh Kenner, *A Sinking Island* (New York: Alfred A. Knopf, 1988), p. 133.

11. James Lord, *Giacometti* (New York: Farrar Straus Giroux, 1985), p. 258.

12. Stanley Sultan, *Eliot, Joyce & Company* (New York: Oxford University Press, 1987), p. 4.

13. Ibid., p. 35.

14. Hugh Kenner, *A Homemade World* (New York: William Morrow, 1975), pp. 5–7.

15. Marjorie Perloff, *The Futurist Moment* (Chicago: University of Chicago Press, 1986), p. 74.

Production civilizes. Edmund Wilson wrote to Stanley Dell on August 6, 1925, about commodities, styles, and social progress: "There is no doubt, however, that ordinary American country and small-town life—with its Fords, movies, real-estate developments, and little flappers with bobbed hair and 'nude' stockings—is a much bigger and brighter thing than it was when I was a boy. It seems to me that it was inexpressibly dreary, ignorant, stagnant, and stuffy then. . . . I take it that a similar change is taking place everywhere else in America and I think it probably represents a real improvement in civilization." From *Letters on Literature and Politics: 1912–1972*, ed. Elena Wilson (New York: Farrar Straus and Giroux, 1977), 125.

16. Maurice Raynal, *Modern Painting* (World Publishing Company: Cleveland, 1960), pp. 139, 158, 203.

17. Perloff, *The Futurist Moment*, p. 46. See also Dore Ashton, *A Fable of Modern Art* (Berkeley: University of California Press, 1991), pp. 88–91, for a sense of Picasso's interest in produced objects that he called "fragments of the real."

18. See the long essay on narrative in Karl's *Modern and Modernism* (New York: Atheneum, 1985), pp. 268–366. This citation from p. 277.

19. Ibid., pp. 279.

20. Ibid., p. 281.

21. Perloff (p.37) cites Germano Celant.

22. Susan Sontag, *On Photography* (New York: Dell, 1973), p. 78.

23. Ibid., p. 91.

24. Ibid., p. 90.

25. See Matthew J. Bruccoli, ed., *The Notebooks of F. Scott Fitzgerald* (New York: Harcourt Brace Jovanovich, 1978), p. 33. This section of the *Notebooks* (pp. 31–55) is intensely conscious of mechanical form and artificial light: "flash-

ing . . . lighted hold of a barge. . . . The Ferris wheel, pricked out now in lights. . . . dock lights. . . . black silhouettes. . . . a building upon a lit-up platform. . . . a movie sign, usually with a few bulbs out in the center. . . . The evening gem play of New York. . . . The nineteen wild green eyes of a bus. . . . silver lines of car track and the gold of the lamps.

26. Richard Hertz and Norman M. Klein, *Twentieth Century Art Theory* (Englewood Cliffs: Prentice-Hall, 1990), p. 252.

27. Ibid., p. 51.

28. Perloff, *The Futurist Moment,* 179.

29. Ibid., p. 181.

30. Dawn Ades, *The 20th-Century Poster: Design of the Avant Garde* (New York: Abbeville Press, 1984).

31. Meyer Schapiro, "Recent Abstract Painting," in *Modern Art* (New York: Braziller, 1982), p. 215.

32. See Hugh Kenner, *The Pound Era* (Berkeley: University of California Press, 1973), p. 30: "In 1919 T. S. Eliot stood in a cave in southern France, experiencing the revelation that 'art never improves,' and soon afterwards wrote of how all art enters a simultaneous order. When Wyndham Lewis writes (*Tarr,* about 1914) that 'the lines and masses of a statue are its soul' (art has *no inside,* nothing you cannot *see*), he tells us that we may confront any art as we must confront that of the Upper Paleolithic."

33. See Raynal, ed., *Modern Painting,* pp. 118; 219.

34. Grover Smith, *The Waste Land* (London: George Allen & Unwin, 1983), p. 9.

35. See Karl, *Modern and Modernism,* p. 277.

36. Richard Finneran, ed., *The Poems of W. B. Yeats* (New York: Macmillan, 1983), p. 210.

37. See the reproduction of "Drawing printed in the notebook published to mark the performance of *Ubu Enchaîné* by the Comédie des Champs Elysées in September 1937," in *Homage to Picasso: Special issue of the XXe siècle Review,* ed. G. di San Lazzaro (New York: Tudor, 1971), p. 25.

38. E. H. Gombrich, *Meditations on a Hobby Horse* (London: Phaidon Press, 1965), pp. 51, 52.

39. Schapiro, *Modern Art,* p. 216. The "new faith in the self-sufficiency of forms and colors" expressed the artist's "view of the external world, his affirmation of the self or certain parts of the self, against devalued social norms" (216–17).

40. Hugh Kenner, *A Sinking Island* (New York: Alfred A. Knopf, 1988), p. 133.

41. Hertz and Klein, *Twentieth Century Art Theory,* p. 252.

42. Schapiro, *Modern Art,* p. 216.

43. F. Scott Fitzgerald, *The Crack-Up,* ed. Edmund Wilson (New York: New Directions, 1945), pp. 30–31.

44. Schapiro, *Modern Art,* p. 215.

45. George Garrett, "Fire and Freshness: A Matter of Style in *The Great Gatsby,*" in *New Essays on The Great Gatsby,* ed. Matthew J. Bruccoli (New York: Cambridge University Press, 1985), pp. 114–15.

46. From *Webster's Third International Dictionary.*

5

Seeing Yourself

■   Characters in *The Great Gatsby* remember advertisements and pose for the camera and go to the movies; they are overseen by an iconic billboard. We first meet Daisy and Jordan theatrically poised, "*as though* upon an anchored balloon," and "*as if* they had just blown back in after a short flight around the house" (10) (emphasis added). Tom is seen poised and posed against the golden windows of his house, and Gatsby is outlined mimetically against the horizon. All but Nick act out their roles and often seem to have scripts in mind. Gatsby, for example, has clearly rehearsed his lines but has not mastered them: "He hurried the phrase 'educated at Oxford,' or swallowed it or choked on it as though it had bothered him before" (52). He is not a very good actor because he often gives way to sincerity. Nick observes that although Gatsby "was picking his words with care" (40) he is fairly transparent—while Daisy gives a much more polished performance in spite of her "basic insincerity" (17). But more than lying or insincerity seems to be involved: character, identity, personality—the subtly different variants of selfhood—seem to be acquired. It is as if all three were to some extent blank or unfilled; and then finished only by the addition of externalities. The major characters have, so to speak, designed their selves around certain scripts and, especially in the case of Myrtle and Daisy, keep referring themselves to themes or even to scenes from ads and movies and other sources of personal identity.

Lionel Trilling said that this was the last of the great novels about the Young Man From the Provinces but it may be the first of the great novels to arise from B movies.[1] It contains a number of Broadway and Hollywood chestnuts: The Poor Little Rich Girl, Flaming Youth, Neglected Wives. There is fiction within fiction:

> Catherine leaned close to me and whispered in my ear:
> "Neither of them can stand the person they're married to."
> "Can't they?"
> "Can't *stand* them." She looked at Myrtle and then at Tom. "What I say is, why go on living with them if they can't stand them? If I was them I'd get a divorce and get married to each other right away."
> "Doesn't she like Wilson either?"

The answer to this was unexpected. It came from Myrtle who had overheard the question and it was violent and obscene.

"You see?" cried Catherine triumphantly. She lowered her voice again. "It's really his wife that's keeping them apart. She's a Catholic and they don't believe in divorce."

Daisy was not a Catholic and I was a little shocked at the elaborateness of the lie.

"When they do get married," continued Catherine, "they're going west to live for a while until it blows over." (28–29)

There is hardly a mass cult theme untouched. This script comes from shopgirl films and scandal magazines—and from movies in which hero and heroine do go way out West for their redemption. When a lie gets that elaborate it becomes, as Walter Lippmann put it in 1922, a public fiction or belief shared by a great many people. Although untrue it is so useful in stating our own relationship to beliefs that it cannot be relinquished—and it has the great virtue of explaining to our satisfaction if not experience at least expectation. The affair has become translated into terms easier to understand than our own circumstances. This particular fiction is not about Home Wreckers (although later in the narrative Tom Buchanan will make up his own version of that theme) or Love Nests. It is about the Poor But Honest Girl entrapped into marriage by A Man Beneath Her and then finding eventually Her One True Love. Obstructed by the least American of religious formalities she will nevertheless Triumph Over Adversity. Following a well-worn path, she will Go Out West and Start Over Again.[2] Myrtle is not alone in making fictions out of facts. We begin to expect theatrics from Daisy when she shows how much she depends on an audience: "She was only extemporizing," Nick says, "but a stirring warmth flowed from her as if her heart was trying to come out to you concealed in one of those breathless, thrilling words" (15). There is that phrase "as if" again, a clue to the relationship of "words" to reality. Nick invites us not only to think about performance but, more important, about whatever is "concealed" by statement—an elegant reversal of our normal expectation. Daisy generally plays to an audience and has a shrewd sense of how she is being received. She often cues applause. And sometimes she cues audience recognition, as in this arrangement she makes for the future of Nick and Jordan: "Come over often, Nick, and I'll sort of—oh—fling you together. You know—lock you up accidentally in linen closets and push you out to sea in a boat, and all that sort of thing——" (18). She has unerringly gone to the movies for an illustration of her intentions. The last phrase, about "all that sort of thing," refers to recent stage and screen practice. Hollywood began early its versions of love gone overboard, and in 1919 Cecil B. DeMille had released *Male and Female,* a shipwreck romance starring Gloria Swanson (who may be the Star at Gatsby's second party to whom Daisy responds so powerfully).[3] Swanson plays the wealthy and spoiled Lady Mary who needs, as this genre demands, to learn from experience. When her yacht runs aground she is cast ashore on a desert island and learns to love her former butler. But there seems to have been more to this version: the old J. M. Barrie "classic" about masters and servants has been updated by the movies in a way that Fitzgerald found disturbingly useful. In its new form, the narrative flashes back to scenes of great lovers from the past, giving Swanson the chance to "play" the roles of love in more than one sense. *She* is on display as a kind of idea of love in herself, entirely narcissistic. Gerald Mast has described the film's empty but everpresent sexuality, its toying with class identity and its ultimate "moral spinelessness" (a DeMille characteristic) when the lower-class lover is given up.[4] The film is a vehicle for Swanson, who represents the irresistibly female—exemplified by gorgeous outfits like that worn by the Star at Gatsby's second party: "flowing gowns and peacock headdress." The movie is all image, and, as Mast states, it plays at love between the classes. It may be a fiction on Daisy's mind.

There is a complex sense of relationship between image and print—and also between short story and novel, novelist, and screenwriter. Fitzgerald had already in "The Offshore Pirate" sent a couple to sea for the discovery of new selves and romance. In that story Carlyle asks Ardita if she is "going to write a movie about me?"[5] It might, she says to him, become a "fabulous story." But, dialogue as public relations notwithstanding, the film made of this short story (released by Metro in 1921) was resoundingly unsuccessful, both critically and at the box-office.[6]

Tom Buchanan, also theatrical, throws himself into the roles of good friend, mentor, citizen, domestic patriot. But although he aspires to something higher he seems condemned to farce: "Once in a while I go off on a spree and make a fool of myself, but I always come back, and in my heart I love her all the time" (102–3). This might have done for Triangle, or run briefly in New Haven. Tom's statement reminds us that in this story self-revelation is often untrue. It is extremely important to realize how often a statement explaining motive or character gives us the wrong information; acts as a psychological defence mechanism; establishes an idea rather than a fact. More and more fictions keep entering the text as the protagonists keep rewriting their past and restating their feelings. The passage tells us how Tom sees himself but it does not tell us if he is right. It may not be a critical option to believe that he is right. The passage means many things: that the complex issues of Tom's life have been and will be reduced in exactly the way he sees them; that what he says contains all the moral awareness he has; *and that it will be the story Daisy finally accepts*. What he says is a self-marketing fiction, but it will be decisive in shaping events.

A moment of allegorical clarity is almost the last thing Nick remembers about Gatsby's second party. He and Daisy have been looking at the strangely mechanistic romance of the motion-picture Star and her director. The narrative splits perceptions: Nick sees the two cinematically, in a series of exposures; Daisy sees a scene that is as real as she requires:

> They were still under the white plum tree and their faces were touching except for a pale thin ray of moonlight between. It occurred to me that he had been very slowly bending toward her all evening to attain this proximity, and even while I watched I saw him stoop one ultimate degree and kiss at her cheek.
>
> "I like her," said Daisy, "I think she's lovely."
>
> But the rest offended her—and inarguably, because it wasn't a gesture but an emotion. She was appalled by West Egg, this unprecedented "place" that Broadway had begotten upon a Long Island fishing village—appalled by its raw vigor that chafed under the old euphemisms. (83–84)

Nick's description of the technology of that kiss endows it with a certain absurdity, which tells us something about Daisy. Nick emphasizes measurement and geometry and that "one ultimate degree" of proximity is a way of stating more than one kind of calculation. The purpose of the kiss is to be witnessed, not experienced.

Daisy's response to the scene suggests something about her connection to Hollywood and its idiom, but it also says a great deal about the author's tactics. Hollywood means not just costume but enactment and distancing; and it offers (the text is virtually literal on this point) the most dehumanized of choices. What Daisy finds lovely Nick has just finished describing as a "gorgeous, scarcely human orchid of a woman who sat in state under a white plum tree" (82). The phrase "scarcely human" is important because of its tremendous psychological implication.[7] We tend to simplify choices in this narrative—between Tom and Gatsby, between true love and false respectability. But the problem of choice may not be the real problem. It may be that Daisy is sexually and stylistically torn between two passions—or that she does not have even one. She admires the Hollywood model of human relationship because it images but does not feel. Enacted "gesture" without experienced feeling allows her to remain focused upon herself.

Naturally enough, Daisy prefers Hollywood, which is not only aesthetically distanced but censored, over Broadway, which is experienced desire. She is necessarily for gesture and euphemism, and against "raw vigor" or direct sexual feeling. Hollywood and Broadway are not only places but states of mind and body. Broadway, Gatsby's realm, is diamond-in-the-navel. It is raw, and it does stand for sex, but also for what ought to be called the life-themes of sexuality. There is constant circulation from Broadway to West Egg and back. A singer thought to be "Gilda Gray's understudy from the 'Follies'" (34) entertains the crowd at Gatsby's first party and is followed by a tenor and then a "notorious" contralto and "a pair of stage 'twins'" who "did a baby act in costume" (39). There is not going to be much costume on either act. The cars from New York "are parked five deep on the drive" (34) bearing uptown society and "theatrical people" (50) to where they belong—Gatsby, "a regular Belasco" (38), has Broadway come to him.

Nick, on the other hand, is drawn to Broadway.[8] After walking along Fifth Avenue and Madison Avenue he goes to Murrray Hill, then along 33rd Street to Penn Station. He feels the sexual urgency of those "dark lanes of the Forties" (47), which lead to "the theatre district." Broadway sends singers and dancers to Gatsby, and it sells its magazines, which are more satisfying than life, to Myrtle Wilson. Broadway is the location of those urgent colors and lights that correspond to romantic and to sexual feelings. Gatsby's new life begins "when he came into Winebrenner's poolroom at Forty-third Street and asked for a job" (133). Wolfshiem, himself "a denizen of Broadway" (58), has "raised him up out of nothing, right out of the gutter" (133). Fitzgerald has a script in mind even for Wolfshiem, who combines the solemnity of bearing witness with crazily interwoven texts of Lazarus and the Good Samaritan, with a bit of Michelangelo thrown in. But these are necessary texts for a story about the creation of a life.

At roaring noon in a Forty-second Street cellar Nick sees Gatsby in his natural habitat. One point that the text makes is that Broadway is the realm of the possible. There, "across the street" (56), is where things have happened stranger but more real than any fantasy about Hindenburg's nephew. The information we get may be veiled (as in the death-and-honor story of Rosy Rosenthal), but it is true.

Before Edmund Wilson came to appreciate the National Winter Garden at Second Avenue and Houston Street, and to compare it with the more elevated revues of uptown, he familiarized the idea of Broadway as city art. In a series of essays from the early twenties, he wrote about the kind of people who went to Gatsby's. There are many tangencies: Wilson writes of the *Follies* and of the West Fifties and of Gilda Gray; he even has a piece on "Broadway in August," in which New York is "volatilized by the heat" and ("Those big movies around Fiftieth Street are cool," suggested Jordan. "I love New York on summer afternoons when everyone's away") those left in the city "seek refrigerated moviehouses."[9] Wilson was more than once struck by the connection between Broadway and himself and Fitzgerald: the *Follies* were a "fantasy" out "of Scott Fitzgerald's novels";[10] and Fitzgerald was a *genius loci*. In "The Delegate From Great Neck" (which appeared in April 1924 while Fitzgerald was working on *The Great Gatsby*), Wilson satirized his reverence for midtown:

MR. FITZGERALD. Think of what it would be like to give parties that went on for days and days, with everything that anybody could want to drink and a medical staff in attendance and the biggest jazz orchestras in the city alternating night and day! I confess that I get a big kick out of all the glittering expensive things. Why, once, when I'd just arrived in New York with a lot of money to spend, after being away in the West, and I came back to the Plaza the first night and looked up and saw that great creamy palace all blazing with green and gold lights, and the taxis and the limousines streaming up and down the Avenue—why, I jumped into the Pulitzer fountain just out of sheer joy! And I wasn't boiled either.
MR. BROOKS. Are you sure you weren't a little hysterical?
MR. FITZGERALD. No: I've been hysterical, too, This was exhilaration.[11]

It is an exaggerated and uncontrolled version of the feelings that Wilson had about Broadway. Wilson senses the connection of Broadway to American dreams: "Ziegfeld's girls have not only the Anglo-Saxon straightness—straight backs, straight brows and straight noses—but also the peculiar frigidity and purity, the frank high-school-girlishness which Americans like."[12] Broadway dreams are uncomfortably sexual and get their literalness from all of our pasts. Wilson is fascinated by the sexual reverence of the audience who know the deep meaning of what they see at girlie shows, its connection to taboo. But at the movies we are not in harm's way: Wilson writes that the most stupefying movie in town is "the Hollywood version of *Don Juan*." Movie love will evaporate your mind when you think of its distance from reality—at the Warner Theater, where the show is playing, there is "a gigantic apotheosis of John Barrymore kissing a girl in the clouds."[13] Fitzgerald writes of Daisy, in love again with Gatsby, saying to him, "I'd like to just get one of those pink clouds and put you in it" (74). From Tiepolo to Hollywood to us, with many stops in between.

Those who come to Gatsby's parties from Broadway are vulgar but to Nick endearing: they come "with a simplicity of heart that was its own ticket of admission" (34). The Broadway people at Gatsby's speak only one language. They are in a constant state of sincerity, running their mascara, falling over drunk, going hopelessly past the limits of style. Nothing about them is ambiguous or—to use Daisy's own term for herself, in the way that she intends it to be understood—"sophisticated." The Broadway people at Gatsby's speak hardly any language at all: his parties are dissonant, full of yells and cries and tears. To see Bert Savoy at the *Follies,* Wilson wrote in August 1923, was to feel "oneself in the presence of the vast vulgarity of New York incarnate and almost heroic."[14] Singing the blues is after all an illusion, but not at Gatsby's first party where a chorus girl "was not only singing, she was weeping too" (42). At his second party truth prevails: after Miss Baedeker has had "five or six cocktails she always starts screaming like that" (83). She is either drunk or Delphic, not insincere. What is unspoken in Daisy's life is heard in the other New York:

> I looked around. Most of the remaining women were now having fights with men said to be their husbands. Even Jordan's party, the quartet from East Egg, were rent asunder by dissension. One of the men was talking with curious intensity to a young actress, and his wife after attempting to laugh at the situation in a dignified and indifferent way broke down entirely and resorted to flank attacks—at intervals she appeared suddenly at his side like an angry diamond, and hissed "You promised!" into his ear. (43)

At Gatsby's there are no euphemisms. This couple offers an obverse view of Tom and Daisy. Either the Buchanans have great resources of strength of character or limitless sophistication, or they feel nothing that needs to be repressed.

Daisy is a southern belle with culturally transmitted mannerisms, including a line about helplessness and gaiety and cousins who are like roses. From the beginning of her life, we judge, she has been given a role to play in life. Nick understands that roles necessarily involve "basic insincerity." He does not understand that Daisy's interpretation of her life and character on their first encounter reveal her *metier.* Her purpose is "to exact a contributary emotion" (17) from her audience.

That is meaningful in a sense that mere play-acting or insincerity—
or being a southern belle—is not. Daisy responds to the Star because
she sees a projection of her own theatricality, and something more important than that. Daisy sees a center around which emotions may be
generated but remain unfelt. She understands the narrative of that ex-
tended kiss. It tells the story of love with the Hollywood ending, our
own form of *Kabuki*. Clinch. Fade-out. Forever after. The script has no
human complications; is a satisfying illusion; makes no emotional demands on a personality that resists them.

To an understandable degree all things human are theatrical, but Fitzgerald has gone to great lengths in order to emphasize Daisy's psychological absence from events, her Hollywood style. When Daisy gives up
Gatsby for the second time we realize that the sacrifice has not involved
much tension. A choice is made and taken; there is much talk but no
action. The same can be said of her first refusal: there are few recrimi-
nations and no visible guilt until the night of the wedding itself. When
Tom proposes and Daisy gives up Gatsby for the first time, the whole
story is told in one startling line: "Doubtless there was a certain struggle
and a certain relief" (118). That is an unusual line to find in a writer of
romance. To write that line Fitzgerald had to give up one of the great
weapons in the armory of fiction, the description of love torn between
two objects. The tactical sacrifice is made because he finds it necessary
to concentrate on another issue. Another passage from the eighth chapter ("She wanted her life shaped now, immediately—and the decision
must be made by some force—of love, of money, of unquestionable
practicality—that was close at hand" [118]) is one of the sources in the
text establishing that although Daisy has feelings she has a very limited
sense of self. The aftershock of the passage about her marriage is the remark that she has decided on the basis of "unquestionable practicality."
But the real explosive power of the passage comes from the desire to
have her life "shaped" from outside. That is why she is theatrical: it is a
way of assuming personality rather than displaying it.

The text is relentless in its coverage of her different roles and their
meaning for her. She is made to comment on and explain all her relationships. When we first see her she plays the long-suffering but loyal wife;
then the good cousin, the glamour girl, the devoted mother (an awk-

ward role) and always the small-town ingenue in the big city. Clearly
she has the quality of "creative temperament" mentioned in the novel's
opening. But what is honorific to the audience is detestable to the narrator. We already know that the phrase means "flabby impressionability"
and will find out that it means personality sequentially falsified.

There are moments in the text devoted to the explication of "gesture" as an expression of role. Think of the extraordinary line expressing
Daisy's intention "to show" her daughter to Nick and Gatsby: "'Blessed pre-cious,' she crooned, holding out her arms. 'Come to your own
mother that loves you'" (91). This is a cruel line, impossible to read
aloud without falling into its hyphenated falsity. The instruction from
text to reader is to extend enunciation and dwell on sounds that parody
feeling. The text is insistent, repetitious: "The Bles-sed pre-cious! Did
Mother get powder on your old yellowy hair?" Among the things that
Daisy wants "to show" are maternal feelings and her own innocent resemblance to the child. It is a remarkable moment, one of those great
"mirror" scenes in literature in which we understand subject through its
object.

Nick does not understand feelings that fail to correspond to facts. Nowhere is he at so great a disadvantage as when he confuses statements
about facts with feelings he imagines native to them. After the first encounter Nick becomes aware—"You make me feel uncivilized, Daisy"
(13)—that there are codes which force the reinterpretation of truths. But
he resists the implications. In the provinces facts are what they seem,
and so are reactions to them. Fact, feeling and action are all of a piece: "It
seemed to me that the thing for Daisy to do was to rush out of the house,
child in arms—but apparently there were no such intentions in her
head" (19). It is not only that her "intentions" fail to correspond to facts
but that they do not correspond to her own stated and imputed feelings.[15]
On East Egg things have adjusted meanings: Tom's adultery is Daisy's
theater. It is, of course, a much tonier theater than the one Nick has in
mind—his own description of connubial duty seems to come from melodrama, possibly from tear-jerkers of silent film, another trace in his mind
of the fictions that tell us what life is all about, and are wrong about it.

When meaning is continually adjusted, then codes become indispensable. We recall that long, intricate dialogue between Myrtle and

Mrs. McKee, which becomes intelligible only "if you know what I mean" (27). The higher the range of civilization the more interpretation. An invitation to dinner is made to Gatsby by "a pretty woman" (79) with Tom and Mr. Sloane. She includes Nick, with special emphasis to indicate her own intentions. " 'You come to supper with *me*,' said the lady enthusiastically. 'Both of you' " (80). But Gatsby doesn't "see that Mr. Sloane had determined he shouldn't." Tom and Nick debate reality and nominalism: "Doesn't he know," Tom says, "she doesn't want him?" Doesn't Tom know, according to Nick, that "she says she does want him?" (81). Even simple meanings have to be adjusted: it is Tom who doesn't want Gatsby; the unnamed woman who is forced to learn that he is unacceptable; and Nick who has to decline his own invitation so that Gatsby won't attend.

No divergence of meaning escapes Daisy's formidable intelligence:

> Tom appeared from his oblivion as we were sitting down to supper together. "Do you mind if I eat with some people over here?" he said. "A fellow's getting off some funny stuff."
>
> "Go ahead," answered Daisy genially, "and if you want to take down any addresses here's my little gold pencil." . . . She looked around after a moment and told me the girl was "common but pretty." (82–83)

The passage gives us more than one kind of information. It is superficially about Tom's predictable libido but that is not the central meaning. He may well like "common" women like this girl or Myrtle or the chambermaid at the Santa Barbara Hotel. And they may well be sexually available, although I think that Daisy means here the absence of style. But what matters more is Daisy's own style. That phrase "genially," so squarely about the difference between feeling and statement, indicates her kind of intelligence. Daisy's theatrical mind discriminates between Tom's lie and the truth, between its own feelings and statements. What Nick calls "euphemisms" play an unexpectedly large role in the *text* as well as in the narrative. It can be dangerous to contravene them. When Myrtle shouts, "I'll say it whenever I want to! Daisy! Dai——" (31), Tom breaks her nose with a practiced movement of his open hand. A love affair begins with "a curious conversation about driving a car" (48).

By the end of the story, when Nick says directly to Tom, finally, "You know what I think of you," Tom is left with a response that is more diagnostic than it looks: "'You're crazy, Nick,' he said quickly. 'Crazy as hell. I don't know what's the matter with you'" (139). Nick is right about Tom, but Tom is right about Nick. There is something wrong about refusing to understand codes.

Encoding and decoding matter greatly in the novel of social mobility. In *Old Goriot* Balzac produced some extraordinary effects from misreading social codes. Rastignac makes the acquaintance of the Comtesse de Restaud who says that she is "delighted" to know him. But his "perception" has failed him, and he does not notice that she is anxious for him to leave, preferably forever. When he finally does exit it is to the assurance that she will always be "delighted" to see him. But as he goes out her husband tells his servant never again to admit him. The first experience of life in the salon convinces Rastignac that "I've just made a mess of things and I don't know how, or how much damage I have done."[16] It has been nothing drastic, simply alluding to the truth. But the first thing provincials discover in drawing-rooms is that conversation has more than a single meaning.

Rastignac accepts the difference between fact and style. He understands that high society is highly theatrical. Nick insists on trying to translate things into some absolute form and condition but is unable to grasp that contradiction is a norm. He keeps on going back over dialogues, trying to stabilize their meanings: "I realize now that under different circumstances that conversation [Gatsby has offered him business in bonds in exchange for his services] might have been one of the crises of my life" (65). The last thing he says to Jordan is about neither love nor regret: "I'm five years too old to lie to myself and call it honor" (138). He has confused truth with reality.

A particular passage takes on this confusion directly. Fitzgerald has given Daisy something that we miss in Gatsby, a talent for explanation. He has also given her a theory on the creation of self:

> She looked at me absently. "Listen, Nick; let me tell you what I said when she was born. Would you like to hear?"
> "Very much."

"It'll show you how I've gotten to feel about—things. Well, she was less than an hour old and Tom was God knows where. I woke up out of the ether with an utterly abandoned feeling, and asked the nurse right away if it was a boy or a girl. She told me it was a girl, and so I turned my head away and wept. 'All right,' I said, 'I'm glad it's a girl. And I hope she'll be a fool—that's the best thing a girl can be in this world, a beautiful little fool.'

"You see I think everything's terrible anyhow," she went on in a convinced way. "Everybody thinks so—the most advanced people. And I *know,* I've been everywhere and seen everything and done everything." Her eyes flashed around her in a defiant way, rather like Tom's, and she laughed with thrilling scorn. "Sophisticated—God, I'm sophisticated!" (17)

After reading this passage, we may think sympathetically of Daisy and indeed we should, but it is really about Gatsby's fate. Daisy has been exonerated in advance. The moral dilemma of the novel does not occur when Tom and Daisy arrange their future lives around the kitchen table after Myrtle's death. It takes place in the passage just cited, at the story's beginning.

Daisy talks about the assumption of character as if it were inherently theatrical. She talks about the general conditions of life as if they excused anything. There are, I think, not one but two great models of conceiving the self in this novel. The first is familiar, a theme in the life of the decade and also of the author: actually to *become* other than you are. The second is of equal interest and importance, to *be* what you are in disguise. There are certain reasons for the coexistence of these themes in American life and in this novel. From the first chapter on, Fitzgerald has been intensely interested in both models—even thinking of them as choices. Nick admits that he wants to "become" a Renaissance man, or that he once wanted to when he didn't understand the limits of ideals.[17] Because Nick and Gatsby make the same kind of choice we tend to forget that others in the story perceive things differently.

Daisy may be more like other women than unlike them. The passage I have cited says plainly that she feels compelled to wear a disguise. I will have more to say about its particulars, but want here to point out her conflict between being what she wants and being what other people want. To be "popular," as Jordan describes girlhood in Louisville, is to live up to other people's expectations. To be the most popular girl in town, here or in Fitzgerald's short stories, is to represent the General Will, really to incarnate it. Fitzgerald's women—Daisy, Jordan, Marjorie, and Bernice—know that popularity is based on illusion. Beauty is not all for his Cleopatras—they have an essentially political relationship to men and to the social order. They know what they are, but even more they know what they *represent*. Daisy is one of the weakest of Fitzgerald's women and must argue from that status. She agrees rather than debate meanings. She has ideas but does not use them. She is extraordinarily intelligent, but defines herself through her relationships with Nick and Tom and "family." Tom talks about "family life" (101), but Daisy lives it. When she is sober—and because she is sober, fully under the authority of the super-ego—she maintains "an absolutely perfect reputation. Perhaps because she doesn't drink" (61). And yet she tells us that she has done everything—meaning, I think, that she has thought about doing everything. When she is "herself" (Fitzgerald takes great care to show her "drunk as a monkey" (60) or in a condition of unconscious truthfulness) she says, at her wedding, "Tell 'em all Daisy's change' her mine. Say 'Daisy's change' her mine!'" (61). This is one of the few times in the text that we hear about Daisy's mind. On the other hand, we hear a lot about her decisions.

At the crucial point of the narrative, torn between Tom and Gatsby, Daisy is said to have neither "intentions" nor "courage." One of these words, "courage," is understandable; the other is not. How can we conceive of a human without intentions? But Daisy has surrendered these and not only to Tom. He only represents the realm of social authority to which the "intentions" of a woman, or of this particular woman are subordinate. From one end of the story to the other Daisy has a magic voice that never says "no."

Daisy seems to be without intentions, and, I think, she is also without a sense of self. Perhaps that should be restated in this way: she is willing to modify her sense of self. She acquires her self, and one of her sources is Hollywood. Two points should be considered about personality and movie selves. The first was made, transparently in 1929 by *Middletown:*

"Go to a motion picture . . . and let yourself go," *Middletown* reads in a *Saturday Evening Post* advertisement. "Before you know it you are *living* the story—laughing, loving, hating, struggling, winning! All the adventure, all the romance, all the excitement you lack in your daily life are in——Pictures. They take you completely out of yourself into a wonderful new world. . . . Out of the cage of everyday existence! If only for an afternoon or an evening—escape!"[18]

The second point has to do with a particular kind or *role* of romantic transformation. To go back to Daisy's reaction to the birth of her daughter: who would voluntarily be a fool? Why should it be advantageous to be a fool? Why should being a fool solve moral difficulties? Finally, where does the idea of being a fool come from? We know that Fitzgerald picked up the phrase from Zelda's reaction to the birth of his daughter.[19] But he adapted it considerably. When he gave Zelda's words to Daisy he went far beyond the opposition of intelligence and stupidity. He describes a personality built, by strategic intention, around the idea of protective innocence. That kind of strategy was visibly deployed all around him. The most direct model for agreeable female stupidity comes, I think, from the movies. The movies in the early twenties had several roles to offer—Daisy wants very much to play Gloria Swanson but will have to settle for Clara Bow. There was a flood of movies in which dumb blondes became a national institution. In these movies women are taught to be theatrical. They get their way (or their man) by trickery, glamour, pouting, conniving, cajoling. One of the most interesting things about these movies is that they project vivacity and happiness, instinct rather than intelligence.

We are fortunate that Clara Bow thought about the contradictions of role. In a 1927 interview she stated, "I know that everyone looking at me on the screen says: 'I'll bet she's never unhappy.' The truth is that I haven't been happy for many, many months. The person you see on the screen is not my true self at all; it's my screen self."[20] This kind of statement has become conventional, an aspect of public relations assuring critics that actresses deserve not only money but sympathy. But Clara Bow is very specific and, in light of the mental depression she went through (and the course of her later life, in therapy and under institutional care) she ought to be taken literally. The "role" of women in this kind of movie was to display instinct. And off screen as well— Constance Talmadge was praised by *Time* (July 30, 1923) for becoming a syndicated cartoonist and creating *Dulcy, The Delightful Dumb-bell,* a title more definitive and more referential than it may appear. We realize that Daisy Buchanan is always exciting and a bit breathless—she has no mind to speak of. And yet Fitzgerald has made certain that we realize she is intelligent. Perhaps the contradiction can be resolved by looking at what movies themselves thought about screen romance. Here is *Photoplay,* a trade journal, in 1921: "Man, even the average college man, will fall in love with a beautiful 'dumbbell' more quickly than with a spectacled feminine professor of psychology. It is not that he fears the intellectual equality or superiority of the woman. He is following the natural instinct to seek beauty. Nature knew more about the promotion of the birth rate than all the scientists that ever lived."[21] It does not take much inspection to deduce that the real comparison is not between science and nature but between opposed social ideas. It states in 1921 why a woman might in 1922 make a certain kind of decision about either "screen" or "true" selves. Marjorie Rosen's history of American film, from which I have cited the above, has something to say about glamorous fools, beginning with Rudolph Valentino's famous 1922 interview in *Photoplay.* Valentino contributed to public dialogue the idea that real femininity was a form of concealment, possibly of actual emptiness: "I do not like women who know too much."[22] It was useful advice for Hollywood, and it seems to have worked rather well for Tom Buchanan. The idea attached itself to film and fiction exotica which so captured the American mind at the turn of decade, the myriad films and stories of "Araby" and points east. Female leads were mesmeric and horizontal. Harem models of identity (advertisements reprinted in *Middletown* describe the audience as composed of "Sheiks and their 'shebas'")[23] were influential. Edith Hull's *The Sheik* was on the Best Seller list for both 1921 and 1922, something *Main Street* could not duplicate. Off or on screen, personality was role; and the kind of role was instinctive. By 1924, *Photoplay* could state that while "the aggressively brainy woman is a horror" it is actually desirable to cultivate "typically feminine intelligence, a subtle hint of knowledge." What follows looks like a blueprint for Daisy Fay: the ideal American girl "must have warmth" and "amiability." She must accustom herself to the fact that "all men like vivacity." "She must not emulate the manner nor voice nor outlook of a man." Finally, virtually all female character can be condensed into "Magnetism! That is the word which tells the whole story."[24] It certainly does for Fitzgerald, who wrote a story about a woman with that title. A national super-ego comes in many forms: we can surmise that the nature of women from 1921 to 1924 was understood ideally to be instinctive rather than intelligent, charming rather than decisive.

Daisy understands all this and can to a certain extent make it work for her. There are advantages to complying with authority. But Fitzgerald has made the issue larger and more interesting. Why bother to endure conflict between self and role? Better to adjust self to role than the other way around. If women are expected to play-act for a good life, then perhaps they should become what they enact.[25] And this essentially is what Daisy does, losing incrementally the demands of her own will and adopting protective coloration.

The many references to the movies throughout the text (some of them almost subliminal) accumulate and eventually direct our responses. The narrative is in certain respects a script. According to Robert A. Martin, "Although *The Great Gatsby* contains relatively few references to Hollywood and the movies, enough remain to suggest that Fitzgerald—even after three extensive revisions—was using the medium as a background reference for the novel. Gatsby's dream of Daisy is one that must be created out of myth and metaphor, and sustained, assembled, and directed much like a silent movie in which events and emotion are symbolized through mimicry."[26] One of the reasons why Daisy is fascinating is that even in the Hollywood firmament she too is a Star, at one point in the narrative located imaginatively above the marquee like that "apotheosis" of Barrymore: "Unlike Gatsby and Tom Buchanan," Nick says, "I had no girl whose disembodied face floated along the dark cornices and blinding signs" (63). The carriage he is riding in with Jordan has just passed Fifty-ninth Street—where "those big movies," like Eden on summer afternoons, send out their lights. Nick's description of Daisy, half myth and half metaphor, was to become a Hollywood publicity dream, "the golden girl" (94); and it would linger, ironically, into the television age. But the story is full of ironies—Daisy eventually does get to imitate Gloria Swanson who, in *Male and Female*, retreats back into her money.

Notes

1. Lionel Trilling, "The Princess Casamassima," in *The Liberal Imagination* (New York: Viking, 1950), pp. 62–64. Trilling writes that transformations of class "represent, with only slight exaggeration, the literal fact that was to be observed every day. From the late years of the eighteenth century through the early years of the twentieth, the social structure of the West was peculiarly fitted—one might say designed—for changes in fortune that were magical and romantic. The upper-class ethos was strong enough to make it remarkable that a young man should cross the borders, yet weak enough to permit the crossing in exceptional cases."

2. Romance repeats itself as farce: Myrtle's dreams may come from movies, but her life has a suspicious resemblance to vaudeville. The essential comic subject of vaudeville is lower-middle-class marriage and, within that, the *hubris* of the American housewife. Eddie Cantor, George Jessel, and many other comedians invented nagging wives for their routine in the vaudeville theaters of New York in the twenties. In vaudeville, housewives sneer at their husbands and men threaten constantly to punch them in the nose. Women make men hate their jobs and nag incessantly for clothes. They can't be trusted out of sight. They come equipped with irritating relatives. The great themes of vaudeville are domestic dissatisfactions: "marriage is an unfortunate institution to which the majority of us resign ourselves; women are fashion-crazy, spend money heedlessly and believe that their husbands are fools," according to Robert W. Snyder, *The Voice of the City* (New York: Oxford University Press, 1989), p. 153. See also Douglas Gilbert, *American Vaudeville* (New York: Whittlesey House, 1940), p. 393 and especially Joe Laurie, Jr., *Vaudeville: From the Honky-Tonks to the Palace* (New York: Henry Holt, 1953), p. 425. The Laurie book reprints some standard domestic-hostilities scripts.

3. For a discussion of the Fitzgeralds and Gloria Swanson, see James R. Mellow, *Invented Lives* (New York: Ballantine, 1984), pp. 181–83; 217. The DeMille *Male and Female* is a version of Barrie's *The Admirable Crichton* (1903).

4. Gerald Mast, *A Short History of the Movies* (New York: Bobbs Merrill, 1971), pp. 137–39. The film is about female style and class envy: DeMille spends "most of his time showing the elegance of Gloria Swanson taking a bath (scented with rose water), the water temperature being checked carefully

by her maid, Gloria striding carefully and sliding gently into the sunken tub. One of DeMille's titles asks why shouldn't the bathroom express as much elegance as anything else in life, and the fact that he is interested in asking such a question is at the heart of what is empty about the film." The year following this film Fitzgerald published "The Diamond as Big as the Ritz" with its bathroom designed by "a moving-picture fella."

5. F. Scott Fitzgerald, "The Offshore Pirate," in *The Short Stories of F. Scott Fitzgerald*, ed. Matthew J. Bruccoli (New York: Charles Scribner's Sons, 1989), pp. 70f.

6. See Alan Margolies, " 'Kissing, Shooting, and Sacrificing': F. Scott Fitzgerald and the Hollywood Market," in *The Short Stories of F. Scott Fitzgerald: New Approaches in Criticism*, ed. Jackson R. Bryer (Madison: University of Wisconsin Press, 1982), pp. 65–73.

7. See Kenneth E. Eble, "The Craft of Revision: *The Great Gatsby*," in *Critical Essays on F. Scott Fitzgerald's The Great Gatsby*, ed. Scott Donaldson (Boston: G. K. Hall, 1984), p. 88: "Fitzgerald recognized that the scene could be used to capture Daisy's essential aloofness which was to defy even Gatsby's ardor."

8. Gatsby is "a regular Belasco" in more ways than one. Belasco typified success through change. He was born Velasco, to a Portuguese-Jewish family in 1853. He made his fortune doing shows with typically American themes— for example, the rise of an ambitious showgirl in *Kiki* (1921). See also the outline of *The Phantom Rival* by William Winter in *The Life of David Belasco*, 2 vols. (New York: Moffat, Yard and Company, 1918), 2:402f. The heroine loses her first love, then marries and regrets her loss. She is ready to fall in love again when her first love appears, but finds him to be "plebeian" and now "tiresome."

9. Edmund Wilson, *The American Earthquake* (New York: Farrar Straus Giroux, 1958), pp. 83–85.

10. Wilson, "The *Follies* as an Institution," in *The American Earthquake*, p. 51.

11. Edmund Wilson, *The Shores of Light* (New York: Farrar, Straus and Young, 1952), 153–154.

12. Wilson, "The *Follies* as an Institution," in *The American Earthquake*, p. 51.

13. Wilson, "Broadway in August," in *The American Earthquake*, p. 85.

14. Wilson, "Bert Savoy and Eddie Cantor of the *Follies*," in *The American Earthquake*, p. 60.

15. See Susan Resneck Parr, "The Idea of Order at West Egg," in *New Essays on The Great Gatsby*, ed. Matthew J. Bruccoli (Cambridge: Cambridge University Press, 1985), p. 67. Daisy "deliberately chooses to embrace certain illusions and play certain roles as a way of creating for herself a sense of meaning and purpose." And, "as far as Nick knows, she exhibits emotion only once." (The last is puzzling: Daisy is often seen crying by Nick or Jordan or "on the verge of tears" [92]).

T. S. Eliot's early poetry and prose endowed the literature of modernism with a sense of emotional and sexual failure. Love is often the description of various kinds of impotence. In 1919 Eliot's "Beyle and Balzac" stated "the awful separation between potential passion and any actualization possible in life. . . . discontent with the inevitable inadequacy of actual living to the passionate capacity. . . . the indestructible barriers between one human being and another." Cited by Ronald Bush, *T. S. Eliot: A Study in Character and Style* (New York: Oxford University Press, 1984), p. 16. "Beyle and Balzac" appeared originally in *Atheneum* (May 30, 1919): 393. The dozens of brief love stories in Eliot's early work are about the paralysis of feeling with a consequent deepening of consciousness. Sometimes correspondences seem to appear, perhaps between Tom Buchanan and Apeneck Sweeney, but Eliot's influence on fiction in general and on Fitzgerald is not a matter of dovetailing characters. After Eliot love is impairment, not fulfillment. The last phrase of Fitzgerald's "The Sensible Thing" is "never the same love twice." It does not apply, although it would seem to, to Gatsby's obsession: it means that love is impossible to maintain in the presence of self-consciousness. The silent scene of Tom and Daisy reconciling at the kitchen table leaves to the imagination two possible arguments, that Daisy prefers old money and assured status, or that she does not want to be in love—with anyone.

16.   Honoré De Balzac, *Old Goriot* (London: Penguin, 1985), p. 87.

17.   Nick describes the ideal of the "well-rounded man" as if it were already part of the past. To a certain extent it was an idea past its time—in 1915 Ford Madox Ford had written about producing "all-round beings" in our culture but the war did so much damage to the idea of Western culture that the ambition to represent it was nullified. See the discussion of Ford's *When Blood is Their Argument* by Michael H. Levenson, *A Genealogy of Modernism* (Cambridge: Cambridge University Press, 1986), p. 144.

18.   Robert S. Lynd and Helen Merrell Lynd, *Middletown* (1929; reprint, New York: Harcourt Brace Jovanovich, 1956), p. 265.

19.   See Matthew J. Bruccoli, *Some Sort of Epic Grandeur* (New York: Harcourt Brace Jovanovich, 1981), p. 160: "I hope its beautiful and a fool—a beautiful little fool."

20.   Marjorie Rosen, *Popcorn Venus* (New York: Avon, 1973), p. 89. I have relied on this excellent film history.

21.   Ibid., p. 83.

22.   Ibid., p. 85.

23.   Lynd and Lynd, *Middletown,* p. 267.

24.   Rosen, *Popcorn Venus,* p. 84. See the analysis of "animal magnetism" by Bruccoli, *Some Sort of Epic Grandeur,* p. 55.

25.   For the dialectic on women's behavior and thought after the war, see

Sandra M. Gilbert and Susan Gubar, *No Man's Land,* 2 vols. (New Haven: Yale University Press, 1989), 2:258–323. See also Sarah Beebe Fryer, *Fitzgerald's New Women: Harbingers of Change* (Ann Arbor: UMI Research Press, 1988) for a novel-by-novel account of change in the status of women.

26. Robert A. Martin, "Hollywood in Fitzgerald: After Paradise," *The Short Stories of F. Scott Fitzgerald,* pp. 127–48.

6

Seeing the Scene

■   Almost every page of *The Great Gatsby* describes movement and cessation. As the book begins Gatsby's heightened sensitivity to life can be "related to one of those intricate machines that register earthquakes ten thousand miles away" (6). The text is always in motion, and the eye is trained to understand the movement of cars and boats and trains; the orbit of the sun and stars; the movement of the body in expressive grace; and the more subtle movement of objects in our perception as we ourselves are in motion. Motion and stillness will often refer themselves to technology, and their perception is in a special way technological. For example, the changes of summer come "just as things grow in fast movies" (7). We will see objects composed and framed, and sometimes through the "flicker" of moving-picture film. We will find it useful to recall the new vocabulary of image and perspective provided for Fitzgerald's generation by D. W. Griffith and other directors:

Panning Shots
Close-ups
Cameos, Vignettes
Dissolve
Camera Angles
Long Shots
Subtitles[1]

The language of technology becomes absorbed into Fitzgerald's tactics. For example, in the opening pages of *The Great Gatsby,* Nick tries to evaluate his recollections, mixing past and present in a way that suggests their dissociation. He states strong sympathies, and also tenuous speculation. But, as he reaches back into the past to tell his story, he allows himself more than one mode of narration. His most ironic mode is his most self-consciously "modern," which allows certain subjects to define themselves. I will concentrate in this chapter on Nick's tactical detachment and on the way that he accompanies his deeply human—and humanizing—narrative with a different kind of telling. He will be as coldly objective as the eye of the camera.

The first major character Nick meets is Tom Buchanan who is suddenly (and literally) embodied through the perspective of the lens. There will be a special kind of perception. What we need to know about him will be provided by visual "objectivity." Nick has us understand Tom without dialogue. But perhaps we do not need dialogue, for this is the age of silent film and it has given us a newly appropriate language.

Detail (heavily edited) has particular meaning. The introduction scene is complex and full of the traces of mechanism. There is first a long pan shot from the horizon to the lawn of Tom's house, which runs "toward the front door for a quarter of a mile" (9); then a momentary halt at the side of the house to establish a new perspective and a different kind of focus. Tom is seen against the line of bright French windows. There is a double framing effect, with his figure first visible on the porch, then with legs apart against the allegorically "reflected gold" of those windows. Nick has described Tom before this scene in the conventional language of prose fiction. But this view of him adds a number of impressions that dialogue and ordinary prose description do not convey. It is insistently pictorial. The distances involved mean something, and complement the glitter of bright gold. Tom's motionless stance also conveys a special meaning. As in silent film, gesture and attitude work to state what words will not. The lens adjustment from the frame's horizon to the motionless, arrogant figure in the foreground is itself a comment. Tom and nothing else now fills the screen. He has replaced—displaced—bay, beach, lawn, and any other visual presence.

The scene changes in a series of maneuvers as a short pan shot is interrupted by two close-ups: "Two shining, arrogant eyes had established dominance over his face and gave him the appearance of always leaning aggressively forward. Not even the effeminate swank of his riding clothes could hide the enormous power of that body—he seemed to fill those glistening boots until he strained the top lacing and you could see a great pack of muscle shifting when his shoulder moved under his thin coat. It was a body capable of enormous leverage—a cruel body" (9). Tom is a body sensed through the application of force by leverage to mass. There is a cubist effect to eyes and limbs, which are out of proportion, out of place, and organically discrete. The pan and close-ups isolate parts of the body and view them as being independently motivated and free from governing intelligence. But something else is going on also, and I am indebted to Milton R. Stern for pointing it out to me: just when we feel the intrusive logic of movie technology, and even when it seems so apt for the description of its subject we sense also a larger meaning. Nick is an old-fashioned man who senses the rightness of borrowing the technique of these modern times. He too is of the modern moment; and no matter his feelings and beliefs he cannot do without its new kind of perception. There is a splendid counterpoint of old values and new modes, suggesting Fitzgerald's sense of the mutuality and also the conflict of the historical moment.

The unsparing camera's eye views the body in tension. An older moral viewpoint is silent, in suspension. "Objectivity" will go even further when the lens (again literally) dehumanizes, suggests the way things now are in 1922. There will be moments in the text when we visualize separate (sometimes separated) body parts in organic disarrangement. There will be hands under automobiles, genuine finest specimens of human molars, a severed breast. The layout of these things is cinematic: a quick, tight focus that establishes them visually but that will not differentiate them from other things organic or inorganic. It is the opposite of Dickens's tactic of animating things without life.[2] Often when the body is displayed in *The Great Gatsby* the lens is silent about its special meaning. The text does not come to our assistance: we lose the distinction between what is human and what is not. Nor does the lens understand the distinction that Nick makes on the novel's opening page between the "normal" and the "abnormal." All it can do is report.[3]

The American Annual of Photography editorialized in 1924 that "photography has at last reached a position where we can truthfully say it has a place in all our lives, whether we are actively engaged in it or not."[4] The lens had a special place in modernist fiction and poetry. Frederick Karl states that "early film techniques—montage, rapid cutting, freezing, speeding up and slowing down, the long shot, the close-up, even flashback and crosscutting—were developing parallel to comparable techniques in the major art forms."[5] He identifies Ford, Joyce, and Pound as particularly affected by film technique and stresses that Griffith is as useful to reading "scenes" as writers. Clearly the effect of these things, especially of montage, was to distance observer from event and to deny sequential, rational order. The world that montage perceives has no familiar interconnections, which is to say that it can't be explained in moral terms. Karl calls montage part of the "very principle of Modernism" because it suggested that "the visible world" could be reorganized.[6]

The close-up in particular allowed for rearrangement of things and ideas. It differed significantly from still-life techniques and, although the idea of macro-focus had been familiar in literature since Swift's examination of the body in the second book of *Gulliver's Travels*, modernism went far beyond the magnification of the object. In Fitzgerald's own case, he had by 1923 acknowledged his *tactical* interest in lens perspective—as well as his sense of text becoming image. The narrator of "Dice, Brassknuckles & Guitar" states, "Now if this were a moving picture (as, of course, I hope it will some day be) I would take as many thousand feet of her as I was allowed—then *I would move the camera up close* and show the yellow down on the back of her neck where her hair stopped and the warm color of her cheeks and arms."[7] Between 1923 and the writing in the following year of *The Great Gatsby* Fitzgerald developed different ways of using the idea of focal length. There are a number of close-ups in *The Great Gatsby*, although not all of them are the same, nor are they treated in the same way. The introduction of Tom Buchanan, the description of the eyes of Dr. T. J. Eckleburg, and the meeting with Wolfshiem combine movie and pictorial ideas. The faces of all three are studies in distortion; and in all three cases eyes are the subject of perspective. In a 1926 essay, Fernand Léger explained why it was essential for the motion picture camera "to isolate the object or the fragment of an object and to present it on the screen in close-ups of the largest possible scale. Enormous enlargement of an object or a fragment gives it a personality it never had before and in this way it can become a vehicle of entirely new lyric and plastic power."[8] Fitzgerald's use of the technique involves more than personality, although that certainly becomes implied. Tom and Wolfshiem are individualized—the latter is, so to speak, all eyes and, like a watchful owl, completes a 360 degree arc "all around" the restaurant. But it would seem that Fitzgerald is concerned with establishing a pattern of disarrangement: Wolfshiem is all eyes; Dr. Eckleburg only eyes; and Tom's eyes have established a quasi-political dominance over mouth, nose, and ears. When the narrative—or the lens—homes in on eyes, breast, hand, nose, or other organs there is dissociation of the whole. Throughout the novel named or viewed parts of the body (Myrtle's "nerves," McKee's "cheekbone," Tom's "flat hand," Dan Cody's "empty face") exist independent of purpose—or imply the absence of relationship. When there is a close-up, for example, of Myrtle's wide-open mouth in death, the new perspective silently states values or their absence. Subjects, with their inherent human dignity, become objects; "*things and creatures*" (139) (emphasis added) become the same.

Nick states his own character in more than one way. We know—and Tom eventually knows—what Nick explicitly thinks of the Buchanans. But we come to know also how Nick perceives things and essences and relationships. What he leaves out is as important as what he includes. What he borrows from the movie technology of modern times is as important as his implied feelings about those times. We are intended to understand the constant, sad, and evocative counterpoint between his largeness of sympathy and the modes that now constrain its statement, and even include his mind and shape his own character.

■

In writing about Joyce and other moderns the photographic idiom imposes itself and we become used to thinking of lens perspective in place of what once was called viewpoint:

> When the Victorian and Edwardian novelists made use of narrative omniscience, they were reflecting a worldview which harbored few uncertainties. The opening scene of *A Portrait of the Artist As A Young Man,* with its sharply limited perspective, is a consciously symbolic act warning us that the old dispensation has irretrievably altered. The change in point of view is both sign and measure of this change in worldview.
>
> The opening scene of *A Portrait* thus puts us on notice that the comfortable Victorian world is no more. Thrust without warning into a consciousness which cannot order the events it observes, which is incapable of distinguishing among levels of truth or even of sorting out its own sensory perceptions, the reader understands at once that he is in a new world, with changing forces and shifting boundaries, with none of the certainty that the Victorians desire

and that he himself has long been accustomed to . . . the symbolic import of this narrative act is inescapable: for a new world a new vision is needed, a new lens to penetrate and elucidate the new reality. . . . man and experience alike are viewed through an unlikely series of prisms and lenses.[9]

There is a striking application of new narrative technique in the great scene in *Swann's Way* in which Mlle. Venteuil is observed through a window "partly open."[10] As in the scene through the pantry window in *The Great Gatsby,* dialogue is displaced by gesture and attitude, and narration imitates reportage. Marcel has awakened on the slope behind the Venteuil house and sees the enactment of a lesbian love affair. But love is not the center of the scene, nor of interest. What happens takes its significance from what Proust calls its "symbolism": the two women have certain "ritual observances" in which the photograph of Mlle. Venteuil's dead father is "subjected to daily profanation." We see what Proust interprets as an act of sentimental sadism performed before the silent witness of the past. Photography establishes the pastness of the past. It is a technology that allows the present always to place itself in relation to its object; and all previous subjects become our object.

One great assumption that Proust makes—an assumption that Fitzgerald shares and that silent film relies upon—is that behavior thought to be unwitnessed will be true in a sense that openly discerned action never can be. The window view and the long lens offer modernism the tremendous convenience of "actuality." We do not need interpretation if we have the use of these perspectives, which is to say that certain modes of prose long familiar to us become unnecessary.

By 1925, Fitzgerald used ideas about perspective, focus, silent witness, and close-up view with more familiarity than his predecessors, and also with more reliance on the audience's contextual knowledge. A number of his scenes experiment with silence. They are mimetic in the way that silent film is mimetic. They display techniques common to fiction and film. Poses will express attitudes and even ideas, as in that first view of Tom Buchanan with booted legs against the bright gold. Even more suggestive of shared technique is our first view of Gatsby in the night. Film and fashion histories emphasize the development and spe-

cialization of gesture in the early twenties: "In the silent movies styli-
zation of both gesture and looks was necessary for narrative, and pro-
moted not only new ways of walking, sitting and using the hands, but
also the development of styles to suit personalities."[11] One reason for
this was the inefficiency of subtitling. In order for the audience to interpret a given scene, a shared pictorial vocabulary had to be invented.
Our first "view" of Gatsby, like our first view of Tom Buchanan, is not
only entirely visual but cinematic, a reminder of the way that romantic
expressiveness was universally to be stated. The case was not that great
numbers of characters literary or actual used Gatsby's special gesture,
but that gesture had become an integral way of stating meaning.

The silent scenes of *The Great Gatsby* have particular framing and
lighting. The text emphasizes movement within a formal boundary with
backlighting, or beams of light, or reflected or diffused light. Characters
do not realize that they are being observed so that (in a story in which
nearly everyone is theatrical) there is no possibility of their putting on
an act. Silent scenes in *The Great Gatsby* may invoke direct comparison
with still or moving-picture photography. I have mentioned that gesture became familiar on screen; and it should be added that gesture was
understood to be a direct translation of feeling. Given the acknowledged
differences between conscious and unconscious behavior a mechanism
becomes necessary to establish those differences. We consent to the
idea—it is a false idea—that act directly expresses feeling and thought.
Freud had already warned that feeling does not *state* itself but *hides* itself.
Causes are never revealed directly by symptoms, only symbolically.[12]
The nineteenth-century novel was more apt to get it right, especially
Dickens, who knew how to depict neurotic behavior. We don't know
about a character like Uriah Heep when we see his writhings; we have
to find out what they mean, and this takes hundreds of pages. With his
own clinical sense Dickens locates meaning in the *repression* of desire.
But Griffith had argued that to see a face by means of a lens was to de-
cipher the *expression* of desire.

Here is one of the most important of Fitzgerald's silent scenes:

> I walked back along the border of the lawn, traversed the gravel
> softly and tiptoed up the veranda steps. The drawing room cur-

tains were open and I saw that the room was empty. Crossing the porch where we had dined that June night three months before I came to a small rectangle of light which I guessed was the pantry window. The blind was drawn but I found a rift at the sill.

Daisy and Tom were sitting opposite each other at the kitchen table with a plate of cold fried chicken between them and two bottles of ale. He was talking intently across the table at her, and in his earnestness his hand had fallen upon and covered her own. Once in a while she looked up at him and nodded in agreement.

They weren't happy, and neither of them had touched the chicken or the ale—and yet they weren't unhappy either. There was an unmistakable air of natural intimacy about the picture and anybody would have said that they were conspiring together. (113)

For a rare moment Tom and Daisy are revealed without dialogue. One reason for this choice of technique is that the text has until now created a problem in epistemology: when Tom and Daisy do speak they rarely tell the truth. It is not simply that they lie to others or rationalize to themselves. They are inarticulate. It is not Daisy's speech that is golden but her voice. Tom is without an explanatory language, a point consistently made when he states ideas. Nick has marked the devolution of his speech into "gibberish." Daisy will often substitute tone for speech; Tom will substitute act for speech.

Much dialogue involving Tom and Daisy is about the falsification of feelings. Daisy knows that anything Tom has to say needs to be decoded, whether it concerns a telephone call or sitting down to dinner at Gatsby's party. As for Daisy herself, the following is even more complex than it looks. We are at the Plaza as the love triangle is explained:

"I did love him once—but I loved you too."
Gatsby's eyes opened and closed.
"You loved me *too?*" he repeated.
"Even that's a lie," said Tom savagely. (103)

The explanation does not explain: confusion is intense, and it is a confusion not only of who feels what for whom but what love is. No wonder Gatsby is startled—he realizes that Daisy has no way of stating the difference between him and Tom. As for Tom, he confuses one of the few truths Daisy states with what he wants to hear her say. Or possibly, in a sudden access of intelligence, he realizes that Daisy is unable to explain her feelings. Which brings us back to the scene of reconciliation, a scene that would founder under the weight of words. To have Tom and Daisy talk about love, about what they feel and understand, would be a tactical error.

Are Tom and Daisy conspiring at that table in the kitchen? The novel's ending might seem to bear that out. But I don't think the scene's importance depends on that kind of cross-reference. Fitzgerald is trying to get two inarticulate and not particularly truthful characters to say something convincing to the reader and to themselves. What they say must be serious, up to the level of the tragic circumstances. But one of these characters can barely deal with conceptuality. What we *see* in this scene would be farcical if it were *heard.* The possibilities (given that they stay in character) are endless but all comic: Tom, if given rope enough, would orate about family life and family institutions; Daisy would make a great many explanations, all charming and some true, about sadness and loneliness and helplessness. The problem is that until this point neither of these characters has been equipped with persuasive speech. Fitzgerald shares the plight of directors of silent film and has to do something to compensate for the absence of dialogue.

Daisy and Tom can be made equivalent to actors: equipped with attitude, pose, and gesture; surrounded by the right kind of lighting and framing; given the props they need. They can participate in a universal language articulate enough for the audience. If we as an audience know about movies then we will recognize the way they feel by the poses they assume; their highly exaggerated gestures; their spatial relationships— and, above all, by their relationship to the genre of reconciliation scenes.

Space has been heavily defined. The first thing that Nick sees is an empty room through a curtain, then a "small rectangle of light," and finally the reiterated rectangular shape of the "rift at the sill." Theatricality is emphasized by viewing the lighted area from the dark and by interposing curtains and blinds. Like Marcel in *Swann's Way,* we have elided normal perspectives and relationships and are prepared to see something objectively true. Tom and Daisy occupy a space that is the equivalent of a stage: the central lit area is their total reality while everything they do is open to interpretation. The first view through the pantry window establishes the components of the shot: figures, table, contents. A separate line of text describes the joined hands—the equivalent of a close focus. Our perspective shifts twice, once from the full scene to the hands, then from the hands to Daisy's face. Although Nick says that what he is describing is a "picture," it is more a sequence of frames. The frames move, with Tom talking and Daisy nodding in agreement.

At the heart of the scene physically and symbolically are the linked hands. They constitute a visual metaphor which had been in use since the early days of D. W. Griffith. Linked hands were part of film "iconography" or moralized composition.[13] Photographs, calendars, stereographs, and silent film had a common vocabulary. There was the seated man whose wife stood to his right, often with her hand on his shoulder; the mother and child in a domesticated version of the Madonna; the family harmony of relatives arranged by size, age, and importance. One important pose for Griffith and other directors was the familial/matrimonial clasping of hands. It had become an "icon" of union—and especially of reunion. In Griffith's domestic drama the clasped hands of a man and woman were highly specific, signifying "the formal expression of order restored after an assault on the family by fortune or fate."[14] In *A Welcome Intruder* (1913) hands linked together show the restoration of a broken family.[15] The pose is used twice in *Swords and Hearts* (1911), first anticipating marriage between a southern belle and her Union admirer, then marriage between a Confederate and his own true love. There was allegory within allegory: in the latter of these scenes "a newly planted field" in the background functions as "a newly constructed icon of stability and order."[16] By 1920, domestic drama on film had made symbolism familiar.[17] It was in common use because the limits of subtitling were soon reached. The weakness of the tactic was its Biedermeier sentimentality; its strength was audience recognition.

In *The Great Gatsby*, the domestic composition is a contradiction of form and feeling. Until then clasped hands in still or moving-picture photography had been an assurance of matrimonial love. The pose had even suggested passion. But Fitzgerald's mode is irony. Nick tells us that the "picture" has an "unmistakable" meaning that is somewhere between happiness and unhappiness. The negative definition forces us to think over what the picture does not show. Nothing could be more in contrast to the cosmic imagery that informs so much of the rest of the text as the content of this scene. It is as if everything real is material. The confined space itself is a rebuke to imagination. Within this scene there are only plates, food, drink, seats, and a table. What we see refers to sentience and appetite. There is no counterbalancing of these values. Visually absent are gestures that might indicate the realization of guilt, or any affirmation of love. Yet the scene has tremendous affective power and I think that what bothers us most is the assimilation of character into materiality. We sense that Tom and Daisy are in their milieu, that the boundaries of their world are "realistic." The "scene" that Fitzgerald has narrated has, in fact, the traditional values of still life; is necessarily reductive. At this point, Tom and Daisy do not need ideas but reveal essences. Realism shows people who are realistic.

There is an intensely composed sequence before this scene, when Nick and the others pass the ashheaps on their way to New York. The sequence is set up by the disclosure that Myrtle and her husband intend "to go west" in their own version of the pursuit of the American dream. Narration begins with a shot of the entire scene or "locality" and proceeds closer in:

> That locality was always vaguely disquieting, even in the broad glare of afternoon, and now I turned my head as though I had been warned of something behind. Over the ashheaps the giant eyes of Doctor T.J. Eckleburg kept their vigil but I perceived, after a moment, that other eyes were regarding us with peculiar intensity from less than twenty feet away.
>
> In one of the windows over the garage the curtains had been moved aside a little, and Myrtle Wilson was peering down at the car. So engrossed was she that she had no consciousness of being observed and one emotion after another crept into her face like objects into a slowly developing picture. Her expression was curiously familiar—it was an expression I had often seen on women's faces but on Myrtle Wilson's face it seemed purposeless and inexplicable until I realized that her eyes, wide with jealous terror

were fixed not on Tom but on Jordan Baker, whom she took to be his wife. (97)

Setting and lighting are the first things established, with the ashheaps providing a backdrop "in the broad glare of afternoon." At the horizon is the billboard with the eyes of Dr. Eckleburg. There is a quick pan shot from one side of the screen to the other. (Nick has to turn his head to see something "behind" him.) Now, much closer to the eye, is another frame within a frame, like the shot at the pantry window. We see Tom and Daisy through the space left between a shade and sill; we see Myrtle through a vertical opening between curtains and a window frame (possibly between parted curtains). The framing is intensely replicated: there is the billboard, the window, the curtained space and finally face and eyes, one enclosed boundary after another. The sequence is dependent on the technology of the "moving picture." If Myrtle is "over the garage," then her eyes are about fifteen feet above ground level. If she is a little less than twenty feet away in a straight line from Nick's eye to her eye, that places her at a distance and angle from which it is almost impossible to discern detail—especially if there is such a "little" space between the curtains. The scene has been described as if a telephoto lens has pursued Myrtle into that exceptionally small (and necessarily dark) space. The human eye does not work in the way that perception has been described because it has a wide-angle view roughly equivalent to that of a 50 mm. lens. It is impossible for human vision to "zoom" from middle distance to close-up with increased diagnostic powers of resolution. Only lenses of greater focal length will "see" things as Nick has described, through progressively nearer and narrower and more magnified fields of view. We get from first frame to last through panorama, still, and then enlargement.

Since Myrtle does not know she is being observed she is free to display her real feelings by facial expression. But that is by no means inevitable, or even natural. In life many a feeling goes unexpressed. But in silent film we *show* greed or lust or jealousy. When Nick says that "it was an expression I had often seen on women's faces," we are left to ponder how many frantic women he has in his orderly life seen—*or how many movies about them.*

When characters of drama are alone they reveal motive and feeling through soliloquy. It is one solution for the unsolvable problem of visibility in even a small theater. The close-up allowed film to depart from this dramatic technique but forced it to develop another equally artificial. Primary feelings like greed or jealousy became visible rather. than explained. Actresses like Colleen Moore (*Flaming Youth,* 1922) and Agnes Ayre (*Forbidden Fruit,* 1922) were famed for their silent expression of emotion. It is startling to see a clip of Colleen Moore (as in her 1988 obituary in the *Los Angeles Times*) because she seems to be working in pantomime. Unlike more modern clips with the face in professional repose Moore plays her role, not herself: her face expresses the sexual energy of flaming youth with almost as much space between eyeball and eyelid as the eyeball itself takes up.[18] There is a standard reason for that, and for the mechanism of Myrtle's description by Fitzgerald: in the movies eyes were thought to be the essential indicators of character and feeling. In a good actress, they would range from "innocent" to "bold" and would be the keys to understanding her ideas.[19] No matter what particular emotion was conveyed, eyes had to be "telling."[20] As in so much else, Griffith was first to establish the correlation of feeling and facial expression: "he seems to have wanted a closer view of the actor's face in an almost magical 'soul-catching' sense. 'Why not move a camera up close and show an actor's full face?' Griffith asked in a discussion reported by Mack Sennett. 'That would reveal his emotions, give him a chance to show what he was thinking.' "[21]

Fitzgerald calls attention to still photography when he describes Myrtle's expression in terms of "a slowly developing picture." He calls attention to movie images when he describes those eyes "wide with jealous terror" that are the trademark of melodrama. But he does more than allude to the new vocabulary of gesture. This particular close-up unites text and script as it shows Myrtle's confusion between life and movies. I will have to summarize a certain amount of movie and social history.

Myrtle has been interrupted not only at a given moment but in the course of her entire fantasy about Tom. Myrtle is what the twenties called a "working girl," a phrase that has by now changed its meaning and itself become the beneficiary of upward mobility. A working girl in the twenties usually worked with her hands (Nick remembers seeing Myrtle "straining at the garage pump" as he and Gatsby drive by [54]). Working girls did not have careers. They did menial jobs, a number of which are described in the 1933 edition of *Recent Social Trends*—and also by the American Film Institute Catalogue.[22] *Recent Social Trends* is grimly realistic and tells us that nearly all women employed in 1920 were in Agriculture, Manufacturing, and Domestic Service. A minority (less than 20 percent) did clerical work and a much smaller minority (about 10 percent) served as staff in the professions. "Working girls" made very little money, and were sentenced to life in factories, farms, and offices. Social change occurred all around them *but not for them in the institutions employing them.* The fascinating thing about this situation was its depiction on screen: all the facts were right, but none of the implications. There was a new audience: "the smart working girl from a lower-class background";[23] and this audience wanted to see itself ideally. Actresses redefined their roles, concentrated on hard-edged, ambitious single women who, in films at least, changed their fortunes. They were in the menial occupations, and the AFI lists them: Grace Davidson was a factory worker in *When Destiny Wills* (1921) and also Bartine Burkett in *Don't Write Letters* (1922); Mary Miles Minter was a housemaid in *Her Winning Way* (1921), as was Colleen Moore in *Painted People* (1924); Mary Pickford was a dime store clerk in *My Best Girl* (1927); Aileen Pringle was a chambermaid in *Body and Soul* (1927). A long list of actresses embodied new aspirations—Louise Fazenda, Natalie Moorhead, Sally O'Neill, Constance Bennett, and Lassie Lou Ahern. They worked on screen as housemaids, governesses, housekeepers, nurses, cooks, dishwashers, stenographers, and hatcheck girls.[24] Because these jobs lead nowhere there was only one way, in film as in life, to get ahead: in nearly all the fictions of everyday life the lower-class girl marries up, either to a handsome hero or a rich boss. They do not, like the early Pickford, stay faithful to poor men. The disparity between fact and fiction was extreme. And it is that disparity that Fitzgerald plays on. In 1931 he wrote scathingly of "the Hollywood hacks" who routinely falsified sex and love.[25] In *The Great Gatsby,* when he shows Myrtle's hopes, ideas, and fantasies, he identifies them with movies, magazines, and advertisements. Whenever Myrtle talks about becoming what she is not there is a connection between her and the enterprise of mass print and visual literacy. Behind Myrtle's fantasy of becoming Mrs. Buchanan is the new history of selves very much like her, movies of working girls who change their lives by marrying big. Naturally, Myrtle wants to believe that she is just like them—that is why she does what they do, which is try on new dresses and new accents and hope to fool the rest of the world. But Myrtle is no Marie Doros or Colleen Moore or Constance Talmadge. What conceivable hope does she have of making her life into a script, of getting her own Happy Ending?

The scene I've cited, with Myrtle at the window, is the last time we see her alive, except for the retelling of the accident by Michaelis. Fittingly, it is a scene of sudden realities. The reason why jealousy is compounded by terror on Myrtle's face is that the moment marks the divergence between reality and her fantasies of becoming a lady. She looks at Jordan (whom she mistakes for Daisy) and understands, finally, that there is no way she can compete with a woman like that. The lens sees Myrtle at the end of her illusions, her own little script about life over. Just like all of those other "frantic" women on screen she dissolves into despair. The moment has its own definition: as Chaplin frequently said, "Long shot for comedy, closeup for tragedy."[26] The lens has been inexorable, moving from horizon to window to face to eyes as it seeks to find an equivalent for objective truth. According to film strategy something serious is implied—not necessarily death by misadventure but the end of illusions. There will be a new awareness of self and its limits, something that might well cause Myrtle to rush out onto the road, to assert desperately by that act that "we were somebody she knew" (112).[27]

The first view of Gatsby occurs at the end of chapter 1 and is structured by lighting, perspective, and focus. Just before the scene is described, Fitzgerald emphasizes the visual quality of the night in which "new red gas-pumps sat out in pools of light" (20). Vision is the only sense addressed. Description begins with a strong "bright" source of direct light from the moon. There is a horizon and gradations of darkness—to make the scene work Fitzgerald has to direct Gatsby, get him to move out of the shadows and into the light. Perception is intensely cinematic: when we see that "figure" with its arms outstretched it is apparently "trembling." It follows silent film in its display of silent feeling. The scene is frozen, and when Nick looks away Gatsby disappears.

There is no other movement except for the wavering silhouette of the cat that first draws Nick's attention, and fixes our own upon the ensuing stasis. We do not yet know what those trembling arms signify, but, conditioned by the rules of silent film, we sense the romantic possibilities. Their movement remains the only expressed form of feeling in the narrative so far. What has preceded—the dialogue of Tom and Daisy about love and birth and self and life and science and art has been mere verbiage. "Would you like to hear?" Daisy asks. "It'll show you how I've gotten to feel about—things" (17). But what follows is the opposite of demonstration. It is performance, and Nick identifies for the reader "the basic insincerity of what she had said." Words and lies seem often to be the same. As a contrast to verbal camouflage Fitzgerald turns often to silent witness.

Here is another passage about feeling and gesture, about another figure standing with arms outstretched. It comes from a book known to Fitzgerald, possibly a source for him: "Suddenly she opened her bared arms and threw them up rigid above her head, as though in an uncontrollable desire to touch the sky, and at the same time the swift shadows darted out on the earth, swept around on the river, gathering the steamer into a shadowy embrace."[28] The gesture is repeated as the boat leaves the heart of darkness: "the barbarous and superb woman did not so much as flinch and stretched tragically her bare arms after us over the sombre and glittering river."[29] Conrad comes before silent film, Fitzgerald has grown up on it. In *Heart of Darkness* narration is true to literary convention and it explains in patient detail the connection of gesture to "uncontrollable desire." It adduces tragedy, suggests the conflict between true and false, savage and civilized. There is a lot of work going on in Conrad's description. It is designed for an audience with textual imagination. *The Great Gatsby* relies on the familiarity of its own audience, after a generation of movies, with the signs and conventions of film. The "focus" is much tighter. There are no large cultural issues in conflict, only the display (for the first time in chapter 1) of real passion. The action caught by the human eye is really action caught by the camera eye. The scene is completely visual.

But vision itself becomes increasingly affected, as in a "night scene" at the end which is "distorted" beyond perception. It has cold and weak natural lighting. There is a formal sense of perspective, with the scene divided between "foreground" action and a massed, indeterminate backdrop:

> West Egg especially still figures in my more fantastic dreams. I see it as a night scene by El Greco: a hundred houses, at once conventional and grotesque, crouching under a sullen, overhanging sky and a lustreless moon. In the foreground four solemn men in dress suits are walking along the sidewalk with a stretcher on which lies a drunken woman in a white evening dress. Her hand, which dangles over the side, sparkles cold with jewels. Gravely the men turn in at a house—the wrong house. But no one knows the woman's name, and no one cares.
>
> After Gatsby's death the East was haunted for me like that, distorted beyond my eyes' power of correction. (137)

The figures in the foreground reiterate earlier passages. The text has many mimetic and also choric figures of drunken women in evening dress. At Gatsby's first party is the drunken soprano who takes the blues seriously, whose face becomes a pictorial representation of confusion. She lapses into unconscious silence. Myrtle and her attendants, Catherine and Mrs. McKee, are in a drunken fog in her apartment; the latter two stumble through the furniture as she lies bleeding fluently. Daisy is one of these figures, lying in her bed before the wedding, drunk as a monkey, before she too lapses into silence. Drunk the last time we see her, Miss Baedeker ("she always starts screaming like that" [83]) comes struggling back from sleep into her fear of dying by water. There is a sequence of love-booze-silence that anticipates death. By the time the last of these women appears, nameless and silent, the meaning has been ratified.

The scene is directed, the narration telling us what the desired effects are, and how to get them, even to the hand dangling over the side of the stretcher and catching a certain kind of light. What are its desired effects? The scene is entirely visual, and it has no dialogue. The lighting does not illuminate; the action goes nowhere; and the eye *seems* to fail to discern meaning. But we "see" through the eyes of a narrator with deep and generous sympathies. This narrator, like us, is a prisoner of the modern moment, implicated in the new sensibility. The impersonal eye perceives a scene that (like much else in this story) invites a deeply moral response. The absence of that response is telling. There is a new technique of seeing things, and it is part of a new moment that has stripped away moral energies. Nick is aware, throughout the narrative, that the way you see things has something to do with how little you can do about them. To see "scenes" through a lens is to be quite morally distant from them. You can object (as provincial audiences often have objected) to the crimes done before your eyes on stage—the history of Shakespeare production is especially rich in catcalls, boos and, sometimes, far from London or New York, in calls for the punishment of Othello and of Lear's daughters. But a film is already in the can, and there is nothing you can do to stop the action. Images are immune to our intentions.

In terms of tactics, the passage, a kind of sprung rhythm in the text, insistently interrupts the narrative. It freezes action, demands that we think of the scene as image. We remind ourselves of what D. W. Griffith had to say about the problem of orderly narration in both novels and in film. He was working on *Enoch Arden* (1908) and had to account for cutting between scenes:

> "It's jerky and distracting! How can you tell a story jumping about like that? People won't know what it's all about!"
> Griffith was ready for all dissenters.
> "Doesn't Dickens write that way?"
> "Yes, but writing is different."
> "Not much. These stories are in pictures, that's all."[30]

The statement might be reversed: the pictures are by now in stories.[31] Technology and writing have an uneasy relationship, even a shared identity. *The Great Gatsby* is aware of this, and in more than one way—it has been suggested that as early as 1920 Fitzgerald began to prepare his stories as scripts for movie production. His prose is infiltrated with scenes having special "effects" of lighting and staging; scenes intended to allow conversion from print to image.[32] *The Great Gatsby* is full of instructions on its own translation.

Notes

1. Seymour Stern, "*The Birth of a Nation:* The Technique and Its Influence," in *The Emergence of Film Art,* ed. Lewis Jacobs (New York: Hopkinson and Blake, 1969), pp. 58–79.

2. See Dorothy Van Ghent, *The English Novel: Form and Function* (New York: Harper & Row, 1967), p. 159.

3. See Leland Poague and William Cadbury, "The Possibility of Film Criticism," *The Journal of Aesthetic Education* 23, no. 4 (Winter 1989), 5–22. The authors observe that it is difficult not only to tell the truth in film but to see it. They review the hostility of film criticism to "merely" aesthetic or analytical modes:

> The hostility runs deep and is intertwined with issues of film authorship and ideology. The following passage from Christine Gledhill captures some of the issues involved: "Criticism deriving from liberal approaches to the humanities tends to treat an art product's fictional structures as providing aesthetic access to the work's truth, which is then evaluated in terms of how it illuminates the world. In these terms conventions and stereotypes can be read metaphorically for their immanent meaning. . . . However, recent neo-Marxist developments in feminist film theory effectively reverse the values of 'real life' and stereotype, changing the project of criticism from the discovery of meaning to that of uncovering the means of its production." As critics unashamedly in the liberal tradition of humanistic study, we indeed endorse what the first two sentences here say we should endorse, although the ascription is intended to be contemptuous (6).

There are two broadly opposed views: that "it is the nature of the system to turn the cinema into an instrument of ideology" (12) and that films can in fact be understood through what they state rather than what they represent. The authors' first citation refers to Christine Gledhill, "Klute 1: A Contemporary Film Noir and Feminist Criticism," in *Women in Film Noir,* ed. E. Ann Kaplan (London: BFI Publishing, 1980), p. 7; the second citation is from Jean-Louis Comolli and Jean Narboni, "Cinema/Ideology/Criticism (1)," in *Screen Reader 1: Cinema/Ideology/Politics* (London: SEFT, 1977), 5.

4. Cited by Lawrence Jay Dessner, "Photography and *The Great Gatsby,*" in *Critical Essays on F. Scott Fitzgerald's The Great Gatsby,* ed. Scott Donaldson (Boston: G. K. Hall, 1984), p. 177. Dessner adds that "The years immediately following World War I were important for American photography. New technologies . . . could be turned to civilian use. The Kodak line of inexpensive roll-film cameras, introduced in 1890, improved by advances in chemistry and

mechanics, became increasingly simple and sure. By 1920, several manufacturers were offering 16mm motion picture cameras for home use. The first Leica, introduced in 1924, boosted the new vogue for smaller and more versatile cameras which used the 35mm film designed for professional motion pictures."

5. Frederick R. Karl, *Modern and Modernism* (New York: Atheneum, 1988), p. 382.

6. Ibid., p. 384. See also pp. 382–83: "What we saw in Picasso's first gleanings of cubism in *Les Demoiselles* implied an early film technique, in the blending and merging of elements with each other which came to be labeled montage. The early development of the stream in Ford, Joyce, and others implies some of the techniques utilized also by film, especially flashback and crosscutting, not to speak of fade-in and fade-out."

7. "Dice, Brassknuckles & Guitar" appeared in *Hearst's International* and is reprinted in Matthew J. Bruccoli, ed., *The Short Stories of F. Scott Fitzgerald* (New York: Charles Scribner's Sons, 1989), p. 238. Emphasis added.

8. Fernand Léger's "A New Realism—The Object: Its Plastic and Cinematic Value" from *The Little Review* of 1926 cited by Miles Orvell, *The Real Thing: Imitation and Authenticity in American Culture, 1880–1940* (Chapel Hill: University of North Carolina Press, 1989), p. 215. As Orvell notes, we get "strange effects" from the new close-up techniques.

9. Morton P. Levitt, "The Modernist Age: The Age of James Joyce," in *Light Rays: James Joyce and Modernism,* ed. Heyward Ehrlich (New York: New Horizon Press, 1984), pp. 139–40.

10. *A la recherche du temps perdu* (1913–27). *Swann's Way* appeared in the C. K. Scott Moncrieff translation in 1922.

11. Elizabeth Wilson, *Adorned in Dreams: Fashion and Modernity* (Berkeley: University of California Press, 1987), p. 169. Movies created "new ways for men and women to move, dance, dress, make love, *be.*" Fitzgerald uses a certain vocabulary of motion and stasis for each of his characters—we particularly recall Tom Buchanan leaning aggressively forward the first time we see him and, in a kind of psychological coda, walking along Fifth Avenue the last time we see him "in his alert, aggressive way, his hands out a little from his body as if to fight off interference" (138–39). However, see next note for the interpretation of gesture. Psychology and film are less in agreement than is often thought. Fitzgerald seems to have depended on film, not psychology.

12. See especially Freud's 1915 essay "Repression," in *General Psychological Theory,* ed. Philip Rieff (New York: Collier, 1963), pp. 104f. Gesture in Fitzgerald (as in the previous note) tends directly to emphasize a fact or feeling or condition. Tom is "aggressive" so he is made to look something like a punch-drunk fighter. But this is a vast simplification of the idea of physical evidence in psychology—and is really a contradiction. Freud states, "We now wish to gain some insight into the mechanism of the process of repression, and especially we

want to know whether it has a single mechanism only, or more than one, and whether perhaps each of the psychoneuroses may be distinguished by a characteristic repression-mechanism peculiar to itself. At the outset of this inquiry, however, we encounter complications. The mechanism of a repression becomes accessible to us only when we deduce it from its final results. If we confine our observations to the results of its effect on the ideational part of the instinct-presentation, we discover that as a rule repression creates a *substitute-formation*" (p. 111). Even symptoms need translation. Freud has bad news for Fitzgerald and the movies: repression is a process. After it is manifested, it changes: "The vanished affect is transformed, without any diminution, into dread of the community, pangs of conscience, or self-reproaches; the rejected idea is replaced by a *displacement-substitute*, often by displacement on to something utterly trivial or indifferent" (p. 114). In other words, there can be no direct connection between a gesture and a feeling when repression is involved. Film has a difficult time handling repression—it is tempting now as in the twenties to make gesture directly indicative of feeling, which is the province of melodrama. In modern film, as in silent film, and on television, villains scowl and sneer to show aggression and tense their muscles; people show affection by holding out their arms. No one has untranslatable feelings.

13. See the discussion of "iconography" by Joyce E. Jesionowski, *Thinking in Pictures: Dramatic Structure in D.W. Griffith's Biograph Films* (Berkeley: University of California Press, 1987), pp. 142–59. I have relied on this book for my discussion of Griffith and of silent film.

14. Ibid., p. 144.

15. Ibid., pp. 166, 169.

16. Ibid., p. 157.

17. See the discussion of Fitzgerald and Griffith by Ruth Prigozy, "From Griffith's Girls to Daddy's Girl: The Masks of Innocence in Tender Is the Night," *Twentieth Century Literature* 26, no. 2 (Summer 1980): 198: "Fitzgerald, along with most Americans, had absorbed Griffith's work for fifteen years before he started work on TITN." For the "messages" of film see p. 201: *A Drunkard's Reformation* (1909) "ends with one of the most admired shots in Griffith's early repertory; the reunited family sits by the hearth, bathed in the glow of the firelight. The scene is not only a technical triumph of lighting (the only light on the trio comes from the fire), but also a perfect symbolic representation of the light, warmth, and devotion that only a harmonious and responsible family life can insure."

18. See the catalog of clips in Prigozy, 204–6.

19. Lewis Jacobs, *The Rise of the American Film* (New York: Harcourt Brace, 1939), p. 410.

20. Ibid., p. 273.

21. Jesionowski, *Thinking in Pictures,* pp. 17–18.

22. *Recent Social Trends in the United States: Report of the President's Research Committee on Social Trends* (New York: McGraw-Hill, 1933), pp. 716–30.

23. Marjorie Rosen, *Popcorn Venus* (New York: Avon, 1973), p. 81.

24. For citation of the AFI catalog see Rosen, pp. 80–81. In real life, according to *Recent Social Trends,* women worked "in relatively large numbers in seven of the ten major occupational classifications employed by the Bureau of the Census. The greatest number, 3,438,000, are in domestic and personal service. There are 1,970,000 in clerical occupations, 1,860,000 in manufacturing and mechanical industries and 1,226,000 in the professions. Trade and agriculture each claim somewhat less than a million female workers, while transportation and communication include something over a quarter of a million" (pp. 716–17). For discussion of the effect of World War I on both literature and society see Sandra M. Gilbert and Susan Gubar, *No Man's Land,* 2 vols. (New Haven: Yale University Press, 1989), 2:258–323. Gilbert and Gubar review the new kinds of work performed by women during and after the war, and the consequent change in their attitude about themselves.

25. F. Scott Fitzgerald, *The Crack-Up,* ed. Edmund Wilson (New York: New Directions, 1945), p. 17.

26. Louis Gianetti, *Understanding Movies* (Englewood Cliffs: Prentice-Hall, 1972), p. 7.

27. Fitzgerald's experimentation with lens perspective and objectivity may be clarified by reference to Miles Orvell, *The Real Thing: Imitation and Authenticity in American Culture, 1880–1940* (Chapel Hill: University of North Carolina Press, 1989), p. 245. Orvell is discussing the use of the camera by modernism:

> For the late nineteenth-century realist committed to a literature of verisimilitude, the camera's presumed objectivity had served as a model of seeing and representation. And, I must stress again, the popular literature of the twentieth century continued to be written, and read, within what I have called the mainstream middle-class culture of replication established by the nineteenth century, a culture that accepted the writer's medium as a transparent one. My subject here is how the new writing in the early twentieth century challenged the comfortable assumptions of the past, raising fundamental questions about form and representation: What was the material of the literary work? the reservoir of established speech, or a new language to be invented by the poet, rebuilt by the novelist? And how much of "reality" in the form of "found language" could be brought into the artwork? How far could words go in embodying the reality of experience? Was there a correspondence between word and thing? How does the writer achieve aesthetic authenticity, how does one reproduce "reality itself" in a world in which modes of vision have been radically affected by technologies of perception? What was the overall

form of the literary work to be? And these questions apply across the literary genres, for the reinvention of writing was taking place within fiction and drama as much as within poetry, and included hybrid forms in between as well. Wallace Stevens, T. S. Eliot, Marianne Moore, e. e. Cummings; Eugene O'Neill and Elmer Rice; William Faulkner, Ernest Hemingway, Willa Cather, Sherwood Anderson—all were dealing with the problem of representation, posing different solutions to the challenge of going beyond realism, beyond the traditional epistemological assumptions of a culture of imitation.

28. Joseph Conrad, *Heart of Darkness* (New York: W. W. Norton, 1963), p. 69. From the edition of 1902.

29. Ibid., p. 69.

30. Jacobs, "D. W. Griffith: New Discoveries," in *The Emergence of Film Art,* pp. 43–44.

31. *The Great Gatsby* is bracketed by the appearance of Erich von Stroheim's *Greed* (1924) and Charlie Chaplin's *Gold Rush* (1925). These titles are in themselves suggestive, but there is also something to note in their methods. Arthur Lennig points out in *The Silent Voice* (1969) that von Stroheim's film was "tinted yellow whenever some symbolic or actual reference to gold appeared" (p. 165). According to Gerald Mast, *A Short History of the Movies* (Chicago: University of Chicago Press, 1981) *Greed* was "most awesome visually" in the depiction of "the endless wastes of Death Valley—a seeming infinity of caked sand and dust under a pitiless, dead sky" (p. 114). Its love affair begins next to a railroad track that is covered with ashes—and beneath an advertisement. Both von Stroheim and Chaplin present insistent moments of awakening in which men and women must come to terms with their character and fate. The two films associate wealth and death realistically and symbolically. There may be more than one way of reading the context of Fitzgerald. The nightmare evocations of *The Great Gatsby* may echo the somber night scenes of the big movies of the early twenties. (As the notes to the preceding chapter indicate, I have used two different editions of the Mast book.)

32. Alan Margolies, " 'Kissing, Shooting, and Sacrificing': F. Scott Fitzgerald and the Hollywood Market," in *The Short Stories of F. Scott Fitzgerald: New Approaches in Criticism,* ed. Jackson R. Bryer (Madison: University of Wisconsin Press, 1982), pp. 65–73.

7

Reading the Past

■ The texts of the past have left their tracks everywhere in *The Great Gatsby*. Its beginnings are said to lie in Scott's *Kenilworth,* Conan Doyle's *The White Company,* and Dumas's *The Three Musketeers.*[1] Gatsby's ancestry has been traced to *Don Quixote* and *Wuthering Heights* and, with more certainty, to the works of Joseph Conrad. Most scholars agree with Robert Emmet Long, who points out that *Almayer's Folly* is about "the hero's futuristic dream set in an ironic time perspective; his apprenticeship aboard the yacht of an old adventurer who has become rich, which marks his initiation into his dream; the young woman who seems to embody, but then repudiates, the dream; the ghostliness of his house, embodying his 'folly,' at the end; the movement from vision to oblivion."[2] *Lord Jim* is about a young man whose Platonic selfhood is twice defeated; *Heart of Darkness* is about the power of feeling opposed to what Long calls "the spiritual emptiness of contemporary society."

Jay Gatsby is delineated by books in different ways. There are the unread volumes in his library which serve as one of his disguises, and which necessarily point to his understanding of ideas. The library itself is "Gothic" and "English" (37), which says something about more than literary ancestry; it matches well with Gatsby's chivalry. But the texts that may be most important in his own story are not usually found in libraries, although they derive from them. Jimmy Gatz assembles his biography from a motley collection of sources. There are those "improving" books and magazines of his boyhood resolutions that echo themes from a great tradition, and also make them much more middle class. There are "success" stories in the background of which this version reminds us. And there are those texts identified by Nick, magazines that allow Gatsby to invent his own biography. Many of these texts belong to the first quarter of the century. In the case of the Horatio Alger stories and other children's literature produced before century's end, they are the living inheritance of that period.

Past and present are constantly intimated by texts, for author as well as narrator. When Nick draws our attention to the texts of Gatsby's biography, for example, he also says something about writing a novel about romantic love in 1924. Gatsby's magazines are the distillate of fake romance. In a crude and derivative way they repeat stories that

Fitzgerald, before the writing of *The Great Gatsby,* found compelling and even troubling influences on his work. Each of Gatsby's claims is said by Nick to be familiar and indeed they are. When he mentions war and heroism, travel and adventure, Oxford and gentility, mournful love and a quest for self, he awakens echoes of Fitzgerald's literary immaturity. Nick may be describing Gatsby's life story, but he is also describing recent cultural history—including Fitzgerald's. Those allusions to the capitals of Europe and the Indian or African bush echo the subliterature of two generations, the escapism and propaganda of Haggard and Henty; the publicly romanticized life of Rupert Brooke. Brooke had given to the young of his generation a fictional identity— and, eventually, just the kind of mass-produced sensibility that Fitzgerald abandoned. Here is Amory Blaine before Fitzgerald's massive change of subject and style: "To some extent Amory tried to play Rupert Brooke as long as he knew Eleanor. What he said, his attitude toward life, toward her, toward himself, were all reflexes of the dead Englishman's literary moods. Often she sat in the grass, a lazy wind playing with her short hair, her voice husky as she ran up and down the scale from Grantchester to Waikiki."[3] Amory echoes Brooke; Hemingway's Robert Cohn echoes W. H. Hudson (whose novel *The Purple Land* is about the "amorous adventures of a perfect English gentleman"[4]); Gatsby echoes Compton Mackenzie. When Cyril Connolly recollected Mackenzie's *Sinister Street* he thought it representative of the new century's wish-fulfillment, a novel for newly literate masses hungering for distinction. This kind of fiction was generically about schoolboy ideals, Edwardian Oxford, first love, and "literature as the pool of Narcissus."[5] That Gatsby gets to Oxford is a nice point, but it is the last point that is of special interest; these books, like Fitzgerald's first two novels, are so much about self-experience ("trying to forget something very sad that had happened to me long ago" (52) means the opposite of what it says) as to qualify, not figuratively, for narcissism. But Fitzgerald began by admiring the novel and the genre, and he had trouble growing out of both. The Mackenzie hero, like Michael Fane of *Youth's Encounter* (1913), is definitively a gentleman, and a product of Oxford. Then there are the *Wanderjahre* so dimly recalled by Gatsby's magazines: "when he left Oxford, he would explore humanity. He would travel through the world

and through the underworld.[6] The combination of "world" and "underworld" became characteristic of mass cult romance: Gatsby's generation
and Fitzgerald's read about Raffles, then went to the movies for *The
Thief of Bagdad*. After the turn of the century Basil Duke Lee and Riply
Buckner dream of being gentleman burglars and going to Yale. It is a
nice combination, because such figures of novels and movies win "both
wealth and the girl."[7] But "The Scandal Detectives," a story written in
the late twenties, editorializes for its own more sophisticated generation: that kind of dream was "a romantic phenomenon lately imported
from Europe and much admired in the first bored decades of the century."[8] In other words, it served while its author grew up, but he grew
out of it. Nick's account of Gatsby shows that he behaves like an un-
reconstructed Fitzgerald. Gatsby may be the most modern character in
the novel, but he is also the least modern. He has been shaped in those
first innocent decades of the new century.

In some ways *The Great Gatsby* is an exorcism not only of the Bitch
Goddess (or of Zelda Fitzgerald's personal and symbolic impact)[9] but
of Fitzgerald's literary past. Gatsby is a romantic whose ideas about
women and the world come from books written before 1922, books
whose vague ideas about love and honor have trickled down into movies
and magazines. Gatsby is not only an exemplary figure but one of those
discarded selves that writers have to formulate.

Before the writing of *The Great Gatsby*, Edmund Wilson had had
something to say about ideas and the novel. *This Side of Paradise* was
unsatisfactory because of ideas—or because of the way that it elabo-
rated them:

> Your hero as an intellectual . . . is a fake of the first water and I
> read his views on art, politics, religion and society with more riot-
> ous mirth than I should care to have you know. . . . I feel called
> upon to give you this advice because I believe you might become
> a very popular, trashy novelist without much difficulty. . . . Culti-
> vate a universal irony and do read something other than contem-
> porary British novelists: this history of a young man stuff has been
> run into the ground and has always seemed to be a bum art-form
> anyway.[10]

To the extent that Fitzgerald reformed and made *The Great Gatsby* reflective of other kinds of texts Nick's criticism of Gatsby is the author's criticism of obsolete styles—among them, his own. The change from all those Arnoldian book lists in *This Side of Paradise* and the psychological deepthink of *The Beautiful and Damned* to the relentless inclusion of jazz lyrics, advertisements, best sellers, scandal magazines, and newspapers in *The Great Gatsby* is deeply reactive. The absence of high culture from a book so largely concerned with the ironies of love is in fact expressive of the qualities desired by Wilson.

Wilson provided his own example at *Vanity Fair* and later at the *New Republic:* he was as ready to write about Greenwich Village and Harry Houdini as about Joyce, Pound, and Wallace Stevens. He accepts "all the unendurable cheapness of an industrial and commercial and materialistic society," and makes literature out of it.[11] Money and bad taste are interesting, and for both Wilson and Fitzgerald can provoke consciousness. *The Great Gatsby* is about fakery in style, from the domestic heroism of Tom Buchanan to the artiness of Chester McKee to the highest and most rewarding level of vulgarity on which we encounter the imagination of Myrtle Wilson. By 1924, Fitzgerald had learned how to make use of Wilsonian material like the way the blues are sung or how announcers talk to a crowd or what food might look like when it is first brought in for a party. And he moved to another level of allusiveness, requiring that his text be read through subliterary texts of other kinds, fragments of ideas that had become inarticulate, adopted by men and women unable to understand them fully. Like Gatsby, Fitzgerald had a readiness for experience; he was enormously hospitable to the materials that came to him from Broadway and mass culture. But he was particularly interested, among these things, in texts that suggested something about the break between past and present; and that lent intense irony to events experienced under their shadow. They objectified the unusable past, hence they had a great deal to say about modern times.

■

Meyer Wolfshiem tells Nick the significant things in his "memory" about Gatsby: "He was so hard up he had to keep on wearing his uniform because he couldn't buy some regular clothes. First time I saw him was when he come into Winebrenner's poolroom at Forty-third Street and asked for a job" (133). Each character sees Gatsby differently, or something different about Gatsby. Wolfshiem, who does in fact know both "world" and "underworld," comes to understand Gatsby as if his "memory" came from the text of a Horatio Alger novel. Gatsby tests the limits of deprivation: "He hadn't eat anything for a couple of days." Yet he asks for work, not food. But still, "He ate more than four dollars' worth of food in half an hour," a titanic accomplishment in the early twenties. Having met his Alger benefactor, a man wealthy and wise in the ways of the world, and having passed his first test, it is only natural that he should then succeed in "business." But the idea of success in both Alger and in Fitzgerald is more complicated than it looks. Like all other ideas or habits of belief, it had changed radically from the time Fitzgerald read Alger to the time he rewrote him.

One of the great things about this part of the book, about the whole association of Gatsby and Wolfshiem, is its definition of success. Wolfshiem invokes little allegories—the manner of the successful man; the various decencies he is bound to uphold; and the rules and limits of trade. He seems, after Nick, to be the character most concerned with the gravity of life. So it is natural that he should confuse upward social mobility with the Creation—not only has he given Gatsby his "start" but he has also "raised him up out of nothing" (133). Wolfshiem's language is metaphorically exact—even in the American Legion Gatsby gets "to stand high there." The authorized biography according to Wolfshiem takes two paragraphs, but it goes ever upward, and not only from rags to riches. Far more than money is involved because Wolfsheim believes in honor. He believes also that bourgeois heroism is equivalent to inherited gentility, and a necessary complement to it. (This is a turn-of-the-century cultural theme, in which a great many books, pamphlets, and magazines tried to bring the values of gentility to the newly literate masses, and it has been analyzed by Mark Girouard, whose work I will reserve briefly for discussion). As Wolfshiem tells Nick at their first meeting, Gatsby could easily be recognized as "the kind of man you'd like to take home and introduce to your mother and sister" (57). The charm of Wolfshiem's vest-pocket biography is its reconstruction of cultural character and its willful confusion of two realms. He wants to see Gatsby as a real Alger hero, of whom it can be said that "he has undergone the discipline of poverty and privation, and prosperity is not likely to spoil him. He has done his duty under difficult circumstances, and now he reaps his reward."[12] Wolfshiem takes it on faith that success is a matter of character and belief. In this he is, ironically, identical to those much above him.

Henry C. Gatz is just as forthright and just as confused. He tells Nick that his son has learned the right bourgeois values about work, study, and the practice of the useful arts. The longest part of Jimmy's day, according to his schedule, is devoted to work. His resolutions are arranged around the words "time," "day," and "week" (135). Because of his attitude toward time and purpose Jimmy "was bound to get ahead." But this has public implications:

> "He had a big future before him, you know. He was only a young man but he had a lot of brain power here."
>
> He touched his head impressively and I nodded.
>
> "If he'd of lived he'd of been a great man. A man like James J. Hill. He'd of helped build up the country." (131)

We can understand why Wolfshiem so easily confuses the different kinds of "business" enterprise. Both he and Henry C. Gatz are in the mainstream, believers in the morality of success. Wolfshiem thinks of Gatsby in the only way he knows how, as a man whose success automatically makes him better while it benefits society. And Mr. Gatz has made exactly the right comparison. Here is what Carol Kennicott has learned from a battery of nine lecturers (including four ex-ministers and one ex-congressman) at the Gopher Prairie Chautauqua about a certain malefactor of great wealth: "Lincoln was a celebrated president of the United States, but in his youth extremely poor. James J. Hill was the best-known railroad-man of the West, and in his youth extremely poor."[13] It is a lovely, deadpan conflation of meanings. The reason why the presumptively honest Henry C. Gatz and the creatively dishonest Meyer Wolfshiem agree on hard work and success is that by the early twenties Algerism clearly covered several interpretations. Perhaps the most interesting thing is that condition of hopeless confusion into which Mr. Gatz and all those ex-ministers of *Main Street* have arrived: Hill really is like Lincoln when enough time has passed, when the great American public is free to interpret things on its own tilted horizon. In fact, Horatio Alger seems to have agreed.

Alger is often invoked by critics, but more than he is read. To go over some of his output is to become aware that he transcended social mobility. He writes not only about success but about its natural enemies, and perhaps that point is where study of Alger and Fitzgerald should begin. Alger had ferocious class consciousness and his stories are full of resentment expressed by aggression. He states ideas that resonate to Fitzgerald's fiction, ideas not only of big futures but also of rancorous opposition to them. Fitzgerald sometimes noted his smoldering opposition to the upper classes, which is likely, I think, to have reached him through Alger. We have been told that, "Like the rest of his generation," Fitzgerald "knew his Horatio Alger."[14] If that is true, Fitzgerald would have known some of the following. A sincere but truly awful poet, Alger wrote this description of the man who,

> Being taught to consider himself, from his birth,
> As one of the privileged ones of the earth,
> He cherishes deep and befitting disdain
>   For those who don't live in the Fifth Avenue
> As entirely unworthy the notice or thought
> Of the heir of two millions and nothing to do.[15]

This is a concretion of Alger's great secondary theme, a theme repeated in nearly all his writings. For example, In *Sink Or Swim* there is a fight, and the rich boy, who loses, "was more mortified that his defeat should have come from Harry Raymond than if his opponent had been of his own position." He is enraged "that a poor boy like Harry should treat with such indignity his father's son."[16] The rich boy in *Struggling Upward* asks his father, "I hope you don't mean to compare me with a working boy like Luke" and then concludes of Luke that "I believe he thinks he is my equal." In this, Alger assures us, the rich boy "was correct."[17]

A dialogue from *Herbert Carter's Legacy* is especially revealing. Another sprig of the local gentry complains about social change: "I shouldn't want the lower classes to get rich . . . they'd think they were our equals."[18] In Fitzgerald's life (as he saw it) and in *The Great Gatsby* there are two great and visible forms of resentment: ambition, and anxiety about it.[19] Here is Alger's version of the war between the two nations:

> "I like to work," said Herbert.
>
> "You do?"
>
> "Yes, only I like to get something for my labor. You expect to work sometime, don't you?"
>
> "Not with my hands," said James. "I shall never be reduced to that."
>
> "Do you think it so very bad to work with your hands? Isn't it respectable?"
>
> "Oh, I suppose it's respectable," said James; "but only the lower classes do it."
>
> "Am I one of the lower classes?" asked Herbert, amused.
>
> "Of course you are."
>
> "But suppose I should get rich some day," said Herbert.
>
> "That isn't very likely. You can't get rich raising vegetables."
>
> "No, I don't expect to. Still, I may in some other way. Didn't you ever know any poor boys that got rich?"
>
> "I suppose there have been some," admitted James.
>
> "Haven't you ever heard of Vanderbilt?"
>
> "Of course I have. Father says he's worth forty millions."
>
> "Don't you consider him a gentleman?"
>
> "Of course I do."
>
> "Well, he was a poor boy once, and used to ferry passengers across from Staten Island to New York."[20]

This kind of Algerism, whether in Meyer Wolfshiem or in Henry C. Gatz, is logical enough: those whom the middle class calls malefactors of great wealth the working class calls heroes. Alger's biographer understands the issues: no matter that Vanderbilt cheated the passengers on that ferry (and probably endangered their lives in the crossing); or that he made a fortune selling rotten timber to the Union Navy; or that he manipulated railroad stock and got to be the richest man in the country by asking no inconvenient questions.[21] A developing country needs jobs and those who circulate wealth are virtuous. The Alger hero necessarily has a lot of Hill and Vanderbilt in him. Like other writers useful to Fitz-gerald he hates rich bullies. He despises inherited wealth. He constantly chews at the edges of the idea of legitimacy. He keeps on asserting that "business," is an innocent preoccupation which needs no analysis itself.

The Alger hero is less simple than he is often perceived. He asks that great question, "Am I one of the lower classes?" He comes to learn not only that success comes through hard work but that it has natural ene-mies. The feckless adversaries of Alger heroes are born to wealth like Tom Buchanan, and they are deeply resentful toward those who aspire to equality. The Alger adversary is often an idler, sometimes a "dandy." He is well-born, the son of the local squire. The other side of gentility is rejection. In *Strong and Steady; Or, Paddle Your Own Canoe* the rich boy continually charges the poor but aspiring boy with "being a beg-gar." There is a fight, and then the following is "sneered" with "vicious" emphasis: "You seem to think you're on an equality with me. . . . Do you think you, a hired boy, are equal to me, who am a gentleman?"[22] The reiterated confrontation seems to have been a psychological model for Fitzgerald, a way not only of explaining himself from time to time but of continually invoking relationships in fiction. The confrontation of gentleman and "hired boy" seems to be on Tom Buchanan's mind when he tells Gatsby, "I'll be damned if I see how you got within a mile of her unless you brought the groceries to the back door" (102).

Alger's adversary figure can be found a generation later, in the school-boy and university novels of the Age of Reform; then reincarnated in the fiction of Fitzgerald, who was one of the last of our writers to deal seriously with the bully of wealth. He was certainly aware that in Alger the adversary's resentment leads to another and matching resentment: Alger invokes Vanderbilt because he takes revenge on inherited wealth. The hero in an Alger novel changes the social structure every time he succeeds. The stories are not only bourgeois myths about work and re-ward but psychodramas of revenge. So, when Rudolph Miller consults Horatio Alger in his tiny provincial library, when Fitzgerald alludes to "half a dozen dusty volumes of Horatio Alger" as a source of inspira-tion, texts are being invoked that do more than identify "the established ideal middle-class hero."[23] Alger is full of bitter truths about the ene-mies of success.

There is a remarkable passage in Fitzgerald's story "The Swimmers" (1929) on American realities. A businessman has become the lover and presumptive next husband of the hero's wife. But the story moves from domestic drama to a larger stage: after telling the hero that he will never get possession of his children because he doesn't have the money for a legal fight the businessman launches into another kind of script: "Money made this country, built its great and glorious cities, created its industries, covered it with an iron network of railroads. It's money that harnesses the forces of Nature, creates the machine and makes it go when money says go, and stop when money says stop."[24] Alger's romance, the romance of capitalism, is clearly a dead issue. In discussing this passage Scott Donaldson argues that the businessman is wrong.[25] But it looks to me as if he is right. Fitzgerald's work is not ironic because his villains are mistaken; it is ironic because his heroes cannot challenge them. His heroes—Gatsby and Nick—have irrevocable loyalties to the past. But during the twenties the entire center of gravity of certain ideas had shifted. Gatsby, Nick, and even Wolfshiem keep stating outmoded allegiances. Hemingway put the matter accurately and, possibly, maliciously in the opening of *The Sun Also Rises*. Describing a would-be writer who went to Princeton and was influenced by romantic books like *The Purple Land* he said that "for a man to take it at thirty-four as a guide-book to what life holds is about as safe as it would be for a man of the same age to enter Wall Street direct from a French convent, equipped with a complete set of the more practical Alger books."[26] Hemingway would give his characters no past at all; the existential present, defining their modernity, is all they have.

■

Certain words are used in *The Great Gatsby* in the consciousness that their meaning has changed in the lifetime of author and protagonist. At the time the novel was written, the meaning of "success" was very much in flux. Gatsby's efforts to rise and Wolfshiem's efforts to legitimate that rise seem hopelessly out of date. Periodical literature from the time when the novel takes place to the time when it was written tells us that there were two broad definitions: a traditional idea based not only on work but on a quality much admired by Wolfshiem, honor; and another idea entirely economic and free of moral obligation. The two definitions were consciously at war. To believe in, say, the rightness of the Alger tradition was to believe, along with *Time* and the *Saturday Evening Post,* that "permanent success" is absolutely dependent on "good will, cooperation and loyalty." The last phrase is twice invoked by a *Post* editorial— "loyalty" is clearly the *sine qua non,* and it may confidently be asserted that "individuals are rarely successful unless they show loyalty toward their employer" (*Saturday Evening Post,* December 16, 1922). Again and again we hear of the noneconomic determinants of success—*Time* takes satisfaction in reprinting the words (August 6, 1923) of Sir George Luna that the determinants of success are "efficiency, economy, honor—these three. But the greatest of these is honor." The idea of "real" success depends on moral energies: there is Henry Ford, the hero as industrialist, who is praised by *Time* (May 19, 1923) because "his chief hobby is work" which makes him such a sterling public example; there is Floyd Dell, the hero as writer, described (May 28, 1923) as "a conscientious workman" who is "forever striving to learn more." *Time* evidently believes that there is a strong sentiment in its readership for the doing of public good, as in the description (May 19, 1923) of Heywood Broun's "gentle sympathy for mankind" which lies behind his own literary success. Each week in 1923 *Time* runs an essay on some hero of industry or letters that is plainly exemplary, a lesson in the true, public meaning of success. In each of these cases "success" means more than profit. It is a word without fixed definition, incorporating many moral qualities. But Wolfshiem seems to know better about honor, loyalty, and all those residual ideas whose time has passed: "When I was a young man it was different—if a friend of mine died, no matter how, I stuck with them to the end. You may think that's sentimental" (133). When Wolfshiem says that, we get the sense that more than one kind of idea from the past has become "sentimental" or obsolete.

There is, at the time the novel takes place, the same conflict in the chivalry of success as there is in that of romance. Periodical literature has a difficult time accommodating to this. Magazines feed on the market for success stories—but there are now fewer readers interested in tradition. Many of them are ready to side with Hemingway against Alger. The idea of innocence becomes blamable; and reliance on tradition or ideas determined by old texts seems like a lapse of self-interest or mentality. In the short story "Irresistible Impulse" (*Saturday Post,* November 11, 1922), William Hamilton Osborne writes of a working girl about to choose a husband. She is herself romantic, but gets sound and pointedly modern advice from a girlfriend: "Don't you know that you can get a fifteen-thousand-dollar-a-year man if you make a try?" Is she a gold-digger? Not if we are to be guided by statistics. *Time* (October 15, 1923) has a brief but important article about the new-fangled science of taking polls; this one about Purdue University questioning its graduates on the definition of "success." It was by now apparent that education was no longer an Attic interlude but part of the world of profit and loss. Purdue, evidently, wanted to find out the correlation between traditional meanings of "success" as opposed to current marketplace interpretations of the term. On the part of the university, the "practical result" of education "was taken to imply 'success' and 'success' was defined as 'the achievement of an adequate and correct ideal.'" *But, on the part of the respondents,* success was defined as "self-preservation (wealth), preservation of the race (valuable service), attainment of a position of authority." There has been an enormous change in definition, although the vocabulary remains the same. Clearly, not only "success" but Fitzgerald's "promise" have taken on new identity in a *Saturday Post* editorial (November 11, 1922): "it is the richness of reward that has made this a land of promise." Alger's moralism, the romantic altruism of Teddy Roosevelt seem no longer to be attractive or realistic. Another poll, this one of high school students later in the decade, is reported by *Middletown:* the determinants of success turn out to be responsibility, independence, and "money income."[27] Periodicals—including those Fitzgerald wrote for—were anxious both to portray themselves editorially as traditional and moral, and to avoid being thrust into the cultural background. They alternate between asserting the morality of success and showing how they resonate to the "modern" and hard-edged redefinition of the idea.

A penalty had to be paid for this schizophrenic conflict. Fitzgerald's own life and the lives of his protagonists might be summed up under the rubric of "Those Wrecked by Success," Freud's influential and deeply provocative essay of 1916. Freud stated in this essay that he was working with literary texts rather than "case-histories." Such texts were as useful as "clinical observation" in defining for us those "censuring and punishing tendencies, which so often surprise us by their presence where we do not expect to find them."[28] Freud goes from Shakespeare to Ibsen to his current practice in this essay, explaining that crises occur not only because of frustrations: they occur also because "long-cherished" wishes are fulfilled. I think the following self-reflective passage from *The Crack-Up* may qualify as the king of text Freud had in mind:

> Charm, notoriety, mere good manners, weighed more than money as a social asset. This was rather splendid, but things were getting thinner and thinner as the eternal necessary human values tried to spread over all that expansion. Writers were geniuses on the strength of one respectable book or play; just as during the War officers of four months' experience commanded hundreds of men, so there were now many little fish lording it over great big bowls. In the theatrical world extravagant productions were carried by a few second-rate stars, and so on up the scale into politics.[29]

Not only was success no longer noble, it was attached to the mass-market conditions suggested by the conjunction of "writers" with "politics" and the "theatrical world." Mencken talks about one of the "stars" in his 1926 essay "Valentino." When confronted in an interview with the obvious intelligence of the actor—and at the same time by his furious resentment and anxiety about his career—Mencken concluded that Valentino suffered from integrity confronted by futility. Valentino loathed his "vast and dizzy success" which he understood to be "hollow" and even "preposterous" because based on the transient, mindless feelings of "yelling multitudes." Mencken stated that, "it was revolting him. Worse, it was making him afraid."[30]

In *Time* (July 2, 1923) Frank Silver, author of lyrics that were sometimes on Fitzgerald's mind, apologized guiltily for his own success. He could not account for it to himself; and he certainly could not account for the popularity of "Yess, we have no bananas." He said (using a phrase that became part of Fitzgerald's cultural vocabulary) that it was "crazy" to see money and success "coming my way" in such a flood. In the early twenties, as in the narrative of *The Great Gatsby,* the idea of success had

become unstable, perhaps even unreal. Nick is torn by opposites in judging Gatsby because he understands the difference between the origins of
the idea of success and its brutal actualities. Nick has a library too, books
"in red and gold like new money" (7), which promise success from
ideas. But, like Tom's friend Walter Chase, you have to swallow your
pride "to pick up some money" (105). To use Daisy's term, one must
become "sophisticated" (17) and adjust outworn ideas. There is an
uneasy correspondence about success between Gatsby and Fitzgerald:
both took "just three years to earn the money" (71) for their transformations, the same three years from their low points in early 1919 to
1922. In order to get that money both determined the course of their
lives. It became an article of faith for Fitzgerald to believe—rightly, I
think—that he was wrecked by success. So parabolically, is Gatsby.

There are other crucial redefinitions. In one of the most insistent
dialogues in *The Great Gatsby,* Mr. Gatz shows a copy of "Hopalong
Cassidy" to Nick and says, "Look here, this is a book he had when he
was a boy. It just shows you" (134). When an author has one character tell another to look, listen or notice a kind of ship's telegraph to
the reader has been activated. One phrase keeps rebounding between
Mr. Gatz and Nick:

> "I come across this book by accident," said the old man. "It just
> shows you, don't it?"
> "It just shows you." (135)

Here is Mr. Gatz on the meaning of Jimmy's SCHEDULE and GENERAL RE-
SOLVES, a meaning that the text has indicated is larger than its statement:

> "Jimmy was bound to get ahead. He always had some resolves
> like this or something. Do you notice what he's got about improv-
> ing his mind? He was always great for that." (135)

Nick has just read Jimmy's GENERAL RESOLVES, which include the reminder to "read one improving book or magazine per week." He feels
morally intimidated, ready now, on behalf of the reader, to "copy down
the list" for his own use. "Improvement" is one of the great prewar
phrases, as meaningful a term for the century's end as "earnest" had

been a generation before.[31] It concerns public character. One of its main definitions is usefulness, and in that copy of "Hopalong Cassidy" Jimmy has singled out "needed" inventions. Nick may think of being a Renaissance man, but Jimmy comes from a more homely tradition. For many years the provinces had debated "needed" ideas: the lyceum circuit brought lecturers to every town big enough for a meaningful audience. It debated abolition and slavery; later temperance and voting rights. Out past the cities, there was the subscription publishing system, which brought salesmen to farms bearing affordable editions of books about "piety, patriotism and history."[32] There were Chautauquas, which so numbed the intelligence of *Main Street*. They bore the creed of "Improvement," which meant that ideas should be useful, have a personal moral effect, and benefit society.

Before the war and in Fitzgerald's childhood "Improvement" was very much in the public consciousness. Under the influence of two men who can without exaggeration be called culture heroes, self-improvement became a creed. The first of these was Robert Baden-Powell, who wrote one of the most influential books of his and our time, *Scouting for Boys* (1908). This was by no means simply a guide to Nature: its purpose was to create civilized character in the mass of the newly literate. Mark Girouard writes that many separate associations were joined in the quest for a specifically Christian gentility. There were socialist groups, groups for the advancement of the working poor, military clubs and sporting clubs. But chief among them was the Boy Scouts, which combined chivalry, industry and public spirit. It is important to recognize the new meaning of the word "gentleman" in Fitzgerald's youth. "A knight (or Scout) is at all times a gentleman. So many people seem to think that a gentleman must have lots of money. That does not make a gentleman. A gentleman is anyone who carries out the rules of chivalry of the knights."[33] *Scouting for Boys* was as much about cities as country. In a recent essay Paul Fussell examines the modern version of this book, which still maintains the old emphasis:

> There is other invaluable advice, applicable to adults as well as to scouts. Some is practical, like "Never use flammable fluids to start a charcoal fire. They burn off fast, lighting only a little of the

charcoal." Some is civic-moral: "Take a 2-hour walk where you
live. Make a list of things that please you, another of things that
should be improved." And then the kicker: "Set out to improve
them." Some advice is even intellectual, and pleasantly uncompro-
mising: "Reading trash all the time makes it impossible for anyone
to be anything but a second-rate person."[34]

The dialectic of *The Great Gatsby* has its cultural equivalents. Its hero
has read two kinds of texts, and his utilitarianism is written down in the
pages of romance.

This utilitarianism is suspended within a larger framework. Gatsby is
at his most American in his transcendentalist quality of imagination. His
assumptions are millenialistic assumptions. The evocations of change
and even of "improvement" have deeply mythical and indeed religious
correlatives. I have been able to write of Fitzgerald's tactical maneuvers
only because so much of the scholarship of the past has firmly established Fitzgerald's strategic intentions. It would not be too much to say
that in the essentials of his alteration of identity, in his subordination
of fact to vision, he is the representative form of what we think of as
national character.[35]

The increasingly secular understanding of "The American Dream"
becomes visible through other lives and texts. The change of self through
vision *and* through nose-to-grindstone "improvement" were momentarily synthesized in the years when Fitzgerald grew up. The second
culture hero I have in mind, Theodore Roosevelt, was president in those
years (1901–9) and one of the most popular advocates of personal and
national change. He was conscious of the power of texts to shape selves
and the relationship was to some extent mutual: the greatest of cowboy
texts, Owen Wister's *The Virginian* was dedicated to him, in recognition
of the themes shared by life and fiction. But there was something more
specific about what Roosevelt represented. Here is William Allen White
sounding very much like Nick Carraway on Gatsby. In 1897, he has just
had his first meeting with Roosevelt, who "sounded in my heart the first
trumpet call of the new time that was to be." And after a second meeting
White said, "I had never known such a man as he, and never shall again.
He overcame me. And in the hour or two we spent that day at lunch,

and in a walk down F Street, he poured into my heart such visions, such ideals, such hopes, such a new attitude toward life and patriotism and the meaning of things, as I had never dreamed men had."[36] White reminds us that "the promises of life" can be more than literary.

White reminds us also that the first decade of the century was romantic in a special sense. There was a well-publicized message of personal mission, personal identity, and national destiny. Nick's visionary hopes and generous admiration have their parallel in William Allen White's politics, and certainly in the cultural politics of Teddy Roosevelt. A recent biography of Hemingway makes the case that Roosevelt's ideas expanded into psychology and literature. He imprinted on the texts of the first decade of the century the conviction that the self could be remade. Michael Reynolds states that "in those days of Hemingway's youth, Roosevelt was in the very air he breathed. His ideas and attitudes had dispersed like pollen, saturating the American scene."[37] The Reynolds biography makes this point about the combination of fictions and identities:

> Raised as he was on the adventure stories of Marryat, Kipling, Alger and Stewart Edward White, young Hemingway tried to make his life fit those fictional models. . . . Teddy Roosevelt had never been one to accept the commonplace experience. He had plucked and lucked his way to national heroics: physical fitness, big-game hunting, exploration, ranching, war, local and national politics. He invented himself, continually advocating his own accomplishments as national goals and virtues.[38]

Roosevelt's ideas were as present in St. Paul as in Oak Park: Fitzgerald thought of him (or thought fit to say of him) that he was one of the heroes of his childhood.[39] The philosophy of Teddy Roosevelt seems to have been made to order for a writer so passionately interested in the heroism of mind and body, who wrote about football and play-writing as if they were both tests of the soul.[40]

Roosevelt had a particular sense of ideas objectified by achieved selves. E. L. Godkin wrote in 1898 that Americans lived in a society "governed mainly by ideas about the distribution of commodities."

There was only one purpose of politics, to "make people more comfort-
able or richer."[41] But money or material improvement were the opposite of Roosevelt's moral strenuousness. He associated wealth with the
power to improve character. And he was fully conscious of the role of
texts in that process. Roosevelt as well as Hemingway can be described
by Reynolds' phrase, trying "to make his life fit . . . fictional models."

The great themes of Roosevelt's life and writings (and of many writings about him) are "Improvement" themes—specifically, the development of the self so that it may better serve the values of Americanism.
Mencken judged Roosevelt to be one of the great studies in American
identity. He was the ultimate self-conceiver, a man who relied on books
for models and who turned himself into an "idea" of himself.[42] It was
not a Platonic idea: what he called "the law of work" was flatly the "fun-
damental law of our being."[43] But, Mencken wrote in 1920, Roosevelt
was the incarnation of possibility. He was fascinated with precisely the
quality in Roosevelt least associated with his privileged class, the desire
for self-transformation. And he was to be valued, Mencken thought, to
the extent that he had the capacity for change, even for transformation.
This goes beyond the usual analysis of Roosevelt's moral authority, and
seems part of Fitzgerald's context.[44] Not the least of points made by
Roosevelt in both life and writings was the effect of childhood texts on
the creation of character.

The date of Jimmy's resolutions is September 12, 1906. It is the summer of Carol Kennicott's graduation and the time of her decision to do
social work, become a nun, be kind to everyone, read Bernard Shaw,
and "enormously improve a horde of grateful poor."[45] Teddy Roosevelt is president, and Jimmy Gatz is learning things of enormous moral
value soon to be outdated.

Jimmy's resolutions are written down in a copy of "Hopalong
Cassidy," one of hundreds of texts produced for boys. The cowboy story
was both "trash" and "improvement." It was escapism, and extremely
poor history of the frontier. But it taught modesty, simplicity, honor,
honesty and reverence for women. In a self-conscious way, in the works
of Owen Wister and his imitators, it called attention to its attenuated
descent from the literature of chivalry and of Sir Walter Scott. This particular cowboy story is one among a number of books for boys and girls

named by Fitzgerald in his various works. He will cite them in order to
state values learned, often passionately, before adulthood. It is the fate
of these values to be tested by adult life—by modern life—and found
obsolete. It is a radical change from what tradition taught. When Roosevelt made his own list of childhood books he was absolutely confident
that they would endure. He could not conceive of altered social circumstances invalidating them. In his autobiography he stated that what he
had learned in the past needed no modification, remained a guide to
thought and action:

> As a small boy I had *Our Young Folks,* which I then firmly be-
> lieved to be the very best magazine in the world—a belief, I may
> add, which I have kept to this day unchanged. . . . Both my wife
> and I have the bound volumes of *Our Young Folks* which we pre-
> served from our youth. . . . I really believe that I enjoy going over
> *Our Young Folks* now nearly as much as ever. "Cast Away in the
> Cold," "Grandfather's Struggle for a Homestead," "The William
> Henry Letters" and a dozen others like them were first-class, good
> healthy stories, interesting in the first place, and in the next place
> teaching manliness, decency, and good conduct.[46]

Roosevelt "greatly liked the girl's stories" as well and in later life made
the point that the "self-education" of children's books was as important for him as Shakespeare or other "masters of literature." The reading list he made up for his own children ranges "from Howard Pyle's
Robin Hood, Mary Alicia Owen's *Voodoo Tales,* and Joel Chandler Har-
ris's *Aaron in the Wild Woods,* to *Lycidas* and *King John." Guy Mannering*
and *The Last of the Mohicans* were balanced by the now-forgotten works
of Laura Richards, Josephine Dodge Daskam and Palmer Cox.[47] Roosevelt thought these stories morally unforgettable, regardless of literary
merit. In that he agreed with that very knowledgeable man of letters,
William Dean Howells, who had a generation before published his own
reading list for boys and reminded his readers in 1890 that many people
are so affected by childhood experience that they "remain in this condition as long as they live."[48] The past, Howells stated, communicates
itself through childhood texts that may have no critical value, stories
"without beauty of invention, without art of construction or character,

without spirituality." But they lay "a spell upon the soul" and the boy who reads them may be "helpless to break from their influence."[49] The particular stories Howells has in mind are those of chivalry, models of an earlier self.

■

In 1895 the first best seller list was compiled. It is interesting in itself to get some idea of what was on that list while Roosevelt was president and Fitzgerald was growing up. One doesn't want to start too far back, but, beginning in 1904, when Fitzgerald was old enough to mess about with books, "serious" fiction by Edith Wharton and Upton Sinclair was hard put to keep up with *Beverly of Graustark, The Little Shepherd of Kingdom Come,* and *Rebecca of Sunnybrook Farm.* The lists were dominated by quests along *The Trail of the Lonesome Pine* and (by 1911) Jeffrey Farnol's *The Broad Highway.* Owen Wister, Horatio Alger and Louisa May Alcott were still household words. Juvenile fiction had become a national institution, and a publishing rubric. It was intensely "improving," a vehicle for the inculcation of civic virtues.

Books for juveniles and books liable to be read by them celebrated the American past and invoked its great figures and types as models of the Rooseveltian present. Such books continually brought themselves up to date, taking account of waves of public interest in cowboys, explorations, and wars. But the characters of this fiction were enough alike to be interchangeable, which could also be said for their beliefs. If you were born as Fitzgerald and Hemingway were near the turn of century, you would have been exposed to a boyhood literature of majority values. You would have accepted a number of views about the world: that cowboys were heroic, that women were sacred, that bravery went with citizenship, and that American history looked pretty much the way Teddy Roosevelt said it did. You would have seen the founders as enlarged forms of yourselves. And you would have had reinforced each time you read such a text the belief that self-improvement and self-transformation were not only probabilities but destinies. Perhaps most important, your views would have seemed destined to endure into adult life, for that was part of the Roosevelt philosophy. The great watershed between nineteenth- and twentieth-century minds was that the latter ceased to believe what they had first been taught. To be modern meant to be educated twice.

Fitzgerald knew that both boys' and girls' books constituted "models" (the phrase is his, from "Bernice Bobs Her Hair") of the unusable past. These models were not in themselves wrong, but they could not be translated into the present. Engaged in the production of a new kind of story about (but not for) children, he went very seriously into the limits of belief. He often in the twenties uses early texts as the first element of a tragicomedy of ideas and identities. One has to give up the past through its texts.

Here is Bernice about to be inducted into the twenties:

"Don't you think common kindness——"

"Oh, please don't quote 'Little Women'!" cried Marjorie impatiently. "That's out of style."

"You think so?"

"Heavens, yes! What modern girl could live like those inane females?"

Marjorie laughed.

"They were the models for our mothers."

"Yes, they were—not! Besides, our mothers were all very well in their way, but they know very little about their daughters' problems." [50]

A certain amount of translation is needed. When Marjorie enlightens her country cousin about the "problems" of girls in 1920 she is talking about money and sex. "Bernice Bobs Her Hair" has begun with a realistic, dismal view of marriage in the middle class. Men and women are yoked to each other on the basis of income and expectation and habit. Some have to wait years for consummation while others, equally unfortunate, are compelled to mate while time allows them choice. "Problems" mean opposed choices: to disbelieve in social rules but go along with them; to ignore them; or to adopt them and make the best bargain possible. Louisa May Alcott is not the only cultural baggage that the "modern" girl has to leave behind. "Like most girls," Bernice had been "brought up on the warm milk prepared by Annie Fellows Johnston and on novels in which the female was beloved because of certain mysterious womanly qualities, always mentioned but never displayed." Neither Alcott nor Johnson have a language for power and sex, nor much insight into one of the large issues of Fitzgerald's story, the expression of sexual energy and aggressive will. Traditional stories (including the modernized versions of juvenilia by Tarkington) imagined a society of boys and girls different from adult society. It was a kind of pastoral, with not much harm in it—threats came, like Injun Joe, from outside. Fitzgerald's children are, however, a microcosm of adult society. Everyone has worries about money and status, and a good deal of self-doubt. There are enemies everywhere, and in the Josephine stories a girl between childhood and maturity is her own worst enemy. Hostility and hypocrisy are givens in this miniaturized society, and are the obverse of "popularity." This is not a place, as Marjorie (who echoes Bismarck on politics) assures Bernice, for "dainty minds." Roosevelt's autobiography of 1913 with its reading lists is hopelessly outdated by comparison with this little worldview of 1920. So is everything that Bernice has learned.

Published in 1928, "The Scandal Detectives" begins with an emphatic contrast between mothers and sons. Mrs. Buckner "belonged to that generation, since retired, upon whom the great revolution in American family life was to be visited."[51] Simply walking across her lawn she is "progressing across a hundred years" toward her own children who belong to the new century. Her own thoughts "would have been comprehensible to her great-grandmother" but not to her son. There is a more specific set of associations in "The Captured Shadow," which begins with Basil Duke Lee immersed in a copy of "Van Bibber and Others," a collection of stories by another (if provisional) hero of Fitzgerald's, Richard Harding Davis. The stories are about Cortlandt Van Bibber, gentleman, boulevardier and *patroon*. He is a few years out of college and into the active life of gentility. Although a fashion plate and model of good manners he busies himself by rescuing maidens, arranging marriages, even restoring an infant to her morally paralytic father. Van Bibber is the quintessential Broadway figure—as that figure is understood by Basil Duke Lee and all the other privileged schoolboys who know that his wealth, leisure, and sophistication are the real ends of their own lives. Among them, I think, is the young Scott Fitzgerald. Van Bibber is associated in Basil's train of thought with the mesmerizing illustration of "three men in evening clothes and opera hats sauntering jovially along Broadway against the blazing background of Times Square."[52] That is to say, he is in the natural habitat of the gentleman. Broadway is the next stop after New Haven.

Richard Harding Davis became an undergraduate hero by creating the college-to-Broadway romance of his own life. The stories that Basil reads were published in 1892 and later assembled in the commemorative edition of 1916 by Booth Tarkington, who was next in the apostolic succession. Tarkington, in a preface well worth our acquaintance, underlined the meaning of the Van Bibber stories and stated why Davis exemplified that new American phenomenon, the big-city hero:

> To the college boy of the early nineties Richard Harding Davis was the "beau ideal of *jeunesse dorée,* a sophisticated heart of gold. He was of that college boy's own age, but already an editor— already publishing books! His stalwart good looks were as familiar to us as were those of our own football captain; we knew his face as we knew the face of the President of the United States, but we infinitely preferred Davis's. When the Waldorf was wondrously completed, and we cut an exam. in Cuneiform Inscriptions for an excursion to see the world at lunch in its new magnificence, and Richard Harding Davis came into the Palm Room—then, oh, then, our day was radiant! That was the top of our fortune: we could never have hoped for so much. Of all the great people of every continent, this was the one we most desired to see. . . .
>
> Youth called to youth: all ages read him, but the young men and young women have turned to him ever since his precocious fame made him their idol. They got many things from him, but above all they live with a happier bravery because of him. Reading the man beneath the print, they found their prophet and gladly perceived that a prophet is not always cowled and bearded, but may be a gallant young gentleman.[53]

Van Bibber is a hero of gentility, but the point about "The Captured Shadow" is that success is not genteel. In order to get to Broadway (or at least to the stage of the Martindale School), a certain amount of creative lying is needed, not to speak of the propagation of a case of mumps. There are texts within texts: Fitzgerald writes a story of a boy writing a script while reading another story by a man who has been the model for both of them. Basil Duke Lee imitates the drive of Fitzgerald for Broadway success, which has been anticipated by both Davis and Tarkington. And throughout all the texts we become aware that the writer is a part of what he describes. In his 1931 essay, "Echoes of the Jazz Age," Fitzgerald recalled Van Bibber as a "utopian ideal" completely out of style—even out of memory—by 1926.[54] Evidently the idea of appropriate "models" of character and style had lapsed. To call "The Captured Shadow" autobiographical is not to come close to its refractions. Basil cannot imitate the more innocent world of 1892, half a generation before him, and Fitzgerald cannot go back to the innocent world before 1916.

The Great Gatsby makes frequent references to that world. Both Nick and Jay Gatsby have been shaped by its ideas; and Gatsby has been specifically shaped by its texts. He has been self-educated by "improving" books and magazines. He believes in the old verities of study, practice, and work. He believes that success comes from work, and personal change from success. As his father sees it, and as most around 1906 would have seen it, the pursuit of success was a public virtue. It is an innocent idea, and innocence is native to comedy—the first notable thing the boy does, at least the first thing chronologically placed in the narrative—is apply good and useful knowledge. Mr. Gatz reflects, "Do you notice what he's got about improving his mind? He was always great for that. He told me I et like a hog once, and I beat him for it" (135). Has Jimmy become too highly mannered for backwoods South Dakota? Or is he right? In either case, the application of a little knowledge is a dangerous thing, just the right idea for a boy's story about the awakening of consciousness in a complex world. When Mr. Gatz tells Nick that Jimmy's list "just shows you, don't it," among the things it shows are other texts that are the causes of the one we are reading.

One of the great, structural ironies of *The Great Gatsby* is that it does not only comment on stories that are its sources; it also follows the lines of their narrative. Like many an American hero its protagonist leaves home and changes his name. It is not a surprise in a literature dominated by Tom Sawyer and Huck Finn. But he comes to exemplify not Twain's but Alger's tradition, and passes three tests of life as viewed by the literature of improvement: he rescues a "successful" older man, he goes to war voluntarily and, after asking "for a job" (133) he proves that he can work his way up the ladder and succeed in "business." After these challenges come rewards foretold by other boys' books: he goes to a great university and then becomes a figure on Broadway. Each aspect of the familiar story is given a twist, however: the Gibson man and Gatsby are on Broadway for different reasons, although both are representative figures of their moments.

The boy is faithful to first love and bases all his life's work on regaining it. In this quest, he demonstrates virtues of what he no longer realizes is the past. These virtues had been formulated—Mark Girouard writes that "American organisations for boys" inculcated "the spirit of chivalry, courtesy, deference to womanhood, recognition of the *noblesse oblige,* and Christian daring" for a long time before the war.[55] He exemplifies some things more than others—but what he does exemplify is startling, at least to Nick Carraway, who understands the difference between gentility and nobility. The boy's success does not in fact occur too late in life for him to win back his first love. But his life is darkened by a hulking bully from a rich boy's school. This bully is easily recognizable because of the way he treats those smaller than himself. He is, like all the bullies of boys' books, a Machiavellian and a liar and has no trouble in blackening the hero's reputation, blaming him for a crime committed by someone else. The hero—our hero by now, because we recognize the genre—is too honorable to reveal the identity of the real culprit. In any case, since it is a woman his hands are tied. He suffers because of his decision to keep honorably silent but is by the end of the story exonerated. The narrator firmly believes that the story has a moral.

When William Dean Howells explains the special province of boys' lives he observes that the bully is a figure of enormous interest for reasons other than his power to harm. In life as in fiction the bully exemplifies the validity of what all boys know, that what he does is always on the side against manliness, community, and honor. In Howells he is a psychological affliction and a test (which nearly all of us fail) in defence of the things worth protecting. A boy's life can be as accurately plotted as a boys' story because there comes a time inevitably when he has to defend himself, or rather an idea of himself. If he wins, so much the better—granted humility. But if he loses, and he will lose most of the time, he will gain at least vindication of that idea. He will know the difference between force and right; and he will have a new and qualified sense of his own character.[56] Fitzgerald reversed this nineteenth-century set of truisms. He has made his bully the voice, self-appointed though it may be, of public values, even of those of "civilization." Tom is certainly the voice of money, power and class. Texts of boyhood fiction and reflections like those of Howells tell us to defy the bully because that defends the ideal. *The Great Gatsby* tells us that there may be ideals, but that the bully makes the rules. He is indeed so representative of the rules that all he has to do is invoke them to win.

Tom Buchanan first appears in the conventional guise of the "hulking" bully whose hand is heavy on those around him. He lies, habitually and strategically. He commits the totemic offense of hitting women. He is not so much evil as infantile. When Nick is through dressing Tom down he assigns him to his precisely right place: "I felt suddenly as though I were talking to a child" (139–40). It is calculated, a reminiscence of the pages of many stories in which the villains are children. In boys' fiction the bully is outside the unwritten rules while the hero represents "civilization." After being thrashed or spanked or otherwise forcibly reformed the bully resumes his place in the community, a sadder but a wiser boy. But in Fitzgerald's fiction wealth empowers infantilism. The Bully and the Spoiled Brat remain immune to anything outside of themselves.

The narratives of childhood infiltrate this text. Alger shares precedence with books and magazines that are also "models" of their kind. We may well ask whether the tactics are large enough for the strategy. But, when Fitzgerald himself was growing up, partly through the instrumentality of books that became for him fables of identity, it was accepted that such books reflected imperatives. Can childhood texts be projected into literature? Mark Girouard believes that such fictions even became part of international politics, and on the largest scale. Here is the year 1914 understood through the language of children's books:

When the moment of crisis finally arrived, most people saw it in terms that were familiar to them from school days, and that gave a chivalrous people no option. They were, in the first place, as Baden-Powell put it, going "to give the big bully a knock-out blow, so that other nations can live afterwards in peace and freedom." Everyone knew that that was what one did to bullies. Even more important, going to war was a matter of honour. For, although the big bully had been throwing his weight about all over the place, the particular nation which he was bullying at the moment was "little Belgium."[57]

We remind ourselves of "Little Montenegro! He lifted up the words and nodded at them—with his smile" (53). Gatsby has been reading something (now a decade out of date) about men and nations that have in common a "warm little heart." I am not sure that Gatsby has invented himself—it looks much more likely that he has assembled himself; and that he has used texts and ideas so firmly rooted in the past that they cannot make the transition to modern times.

Notes

1. See Robert E. Morsberger, "The Romantic Ancestry of *The Great Gatsby*," *Fitzgerald/Hemingway Annual* (1973): 119–30. Morsberger discusses the mix of classics and pot-boilers that interested Fitzgerald as a boy, among them books by Rafael Sabatini, Jeffrey Farnol, Anthony Hope, and Jack London. He mentions also movies based on the popular melodrama *If I Were King* (1901) about "The disreputable vagabond who becomes a nobleman and wins the lady" (p. 124).

2. Robert Emmet Long, *The Achieving of The Great Gatsby* (Lewisburg: Bucknell University Press, 1979), p. 118.

3. F. Scott Fitzgerald, *This Side of Paradise* (New York: Collier Macmillan, 1920), p. 231.

4. Ernest Hemingway, *The Sun Also Rises* (New York: Charles Scribner's Sons, 1926), p. 9.

5. Cited by Long, p. 22. From Cyril Connolly's *Enemies of Promise* (Boston: Little, Brown & Co., 1939), p. 39.

6. Compton Mackenzie, *Youth's Encounter* (New York: D. Appleton and Company, 1913), pp. 501–2.

7. Gerald Mast's description of Douglas Fairbanks in the 1923 film. See *A Short History of the Movies* (Indianapolis: Bobbs Merrill, 1971), p. 136.

8. Malcolm Cowley, ed., *The Stories of F. Scott Fitzgerald* (New York: Charles Scribner's Sons, 1951), p. 311.

9. According to Matthew J. Bruccoli, *Some Sort of Epic Grandeur* (New York: Harcourt Brace Jovanovich, 1981), p. 204, "The novel allowed Fitzgerald to dramatize the most powerful experiences in his love for Zelda: his courtship in 1918, the break in 1919, his triumphant restoration in 1920 (with its attendant financial rewards), and her betrayal in 1924. It is not known how much of *The Great Gatsby* had been written before the July 1924 Jozan crisis." See also James R. Mellow, *Invented Lives* (New York: Ballantine Books, 1986), p. 206. Zelda's affair with Edouard Jozan may or may not have taken place, and "the whole episode, which is central to the story of the Fitzgeralds, is so woven round with a cocoon of fiction and fantasy that it is impossible to know what is authentic and what is invented."

10. The letter from Wilson is in Andrew Turnbull, *Scott Fitzgerald* (New York: Charles Scribner's Sons, 1962), p. 103.

11. Sherman Paul, *Edmund Wilson: A Study of Literary Vocation in Our Time* (Urbana: University of Illinois Press, 1965), p. 38. See the brief assessment of Wilson by Mellow, pp. 96–99, which centers on his recording conversation and details of dress around Broadway.

12. Cited from Horatio Alger's *Herbert Carter's Legacy* by Edwin P. Hoyt in *Horatio's Boys: The Life and Works of Horatio Alger, Jr.* (Radnor, Pennsylvania: Chilton Book Company, 1974), p. 168. *Herbert Carter's Legacy* was first published in 1875.

13. Sinclair Lewis, *Main Street,* (New York: Signet, 1980), p. 232. First edition 1920.

14. Henry Dan Piper, *F. Scott Fitzgerald: A Critical Portrait* (New York: Holt, Rinehart & Winston, 1965), pp. 123–124.

15. *Alger Street: The Poetry of Horatio Alger, Jr.,* ed. Gilbert K. Westgard II (Boston: J. S. Canner, 1964), p. 15.

16. Horatio Alger, Jr., *Sink Or Swim* (Chicago: M. A. Donohue, n.d.), p. 59. First published 1870.

17. Horatio Alger, Jr., *Ragged Dick and Struggling Upward,* ed. Carl Bode (New York: Viking Penguin, 1985), pp. 221–22. *Struggling Upward* was first published in 1890.

18. Cited by Hoyt, *Horatio's Boys,* p. 161.

19. See for example Mellow, p. 179: "Fitzgerald bitterly bemoaned his failure to get overseas, his inability to live up to the men who had the wealth and the social advantages. 'I was always trying to be one of them! That's worse than being nothing at all.'" There is a full-scale study of the subject by Scott Donaldson, "Money and Marriage in Fitzgerald's Stories," in *The Short Stories*

of F. Scott Fitzgerald: New Approaches in Criticism, ed. Jackson R. Bryer (Madison: University of Wisconsin Press, 1982), pp. 75–88. Donaldson repeats Fitzgerald's self-assessment of "always" being "a poor boy in a rich town; a poor boy in a rich boy's school; a poor boy in a rich man's club at Princeton" and, above all, a poor boy in love with a rich girl."

20. Cited by Hoyt, *Horatio's Boys,* p. 160.

21. This is a muckraking interpretation as stated by Hoyt, p. 161.

22. Horatio Alger, Jr., *Strong and Steady; Or, Paddle Your Own Canoe* (Boston: Loring, 1871), p. 111. For the female side of the issue see *Adrift in New York* (New York: Hurst and Co., n.d.), p. 47 (1904). The heroine has been disinherited:

> "Are you going to work for a living, Miss Florence?" asked Jane, horrified.
>
> "I must, Jane."
>
> "It's a great shame—you, a lady born."

23. See Piper, *F. Scott Fitzgerald,* pp. 123–24. According to Piper, "It was hardly necessary for Fitzgerald to know the writings of Alger or Franklin to have been familiar with their philosophy of business success. Their maxims were promulgated weekly in the pages of popular magazines like *The Saturday Evening Post.* . . . In 'Absolution,' Rudolph Miller's tiny library consists exclusively of that authors's works." Piper adds that in Fitzgerald's "Forging Ahead" the hero is reading Alger's *Bound to Rise.* Algerism is often interpreted as if it meant only success. But Alger texts are more complex than criticism about them. The Alger hero must avoid the shame and guilt that naturally go with poverty. He has to fight his own desires. He has to emulate men like Vanderbilt who combined success with gross dishonesty—or normal business methods. He has enemies in the American aristocracy. He has to restrain his aggression. He has to fulfill a public role. He has to survive class jealousy and hatred. The world he lives in is an adversary world and does not grant status to success unless forced to.

24. Matthew J. Bruccoli, ed., *The Short Stories of F. Scott Fitzgerald: A New Collection* (New York: Charles Scribner's Sons, 1989), pp. 495–512.

25. Scott Donaldson, "Money and Marriage in Fitzgerald's Stories," p. 87.

26. Hemingway, *The Sun Also Rises,* p. 9.

27. Robert S. Lynd and Helen Merrell Lynd, *Middletown* (New York: Harcourt Brace Jovanovich, 1929), p. 65. The Lynds note that in answer to the "extreme statement" that "it is entirely the fault of a man himself if he does not succeed" there was an enormous "thirty-four per cent" agreement.

28. Sigmund Freud, "Some Character-Types Met with in Psychoanalytic Work," *Character and Culture,* ed. Phillip Reiff (New York: Collier, 1963), pp. 157f. This longer essay contains its oft-reprinted part, "Those Wrecked by Success."

29. F. Scott Fitzgerald, "Echoes of the Jazz Age, in *The Crack-Up,* ed. Edmund Wilson (New York: New Directions, 1945), p. 22.

30. H. L. Mencken, *A Mencken Chrestomathy* (New York: Vintage, 1982), pp. 238–83.

31. See the important discussion of nineteenth-century "earnestness" by Geoffrey Tillotson, *A View of Victorian Literature* (Oxford: Clarendon Press, 1978), pp. 23–54.

32. See Justin Kaplan, *Mr. Clemens and Mark Twain* (New York: Simon and Schuster, 1982), pp. 61–62; 84–88. According to Elisha Bliss, Jr., managing director of the American Publishing Company, the subscription book was "the people's book." That may have been a diplomatic way of saying what most literary editors thought, who "tended to ignore and resent subscription books as subliterature."

33. *Scouting for Boys* cited by Mark Girouard, *The Return to Camelot: Chivalry and the English Gentleman* (New Haven: Yale University Press, 1981), pp. 220–93.

34. Paul Fussell, *The Boy Scout Handbook and Other Observations* (New York: Oxford University Press, 1982), pp. 6–7.

35. Two collections of essays elaborate the mythical and millenial meanings of the text: see *Twentieth Century Interpretations of The Great Gatsby,* ed. Ernest Lockridge (Englewood Cliffs: Prentice-Hall, 1968) and especially the "History-Myth-Meaning" section of Scott Donaldson, ed., *Critical Essays on F. Scott Fitzgerald's The Great Gatsby* (Boston: G. K. Hall, 1984), pp. 215–58.

36. William A. White, *The Autobiography of William Allen White* (New York: Macmillan, 1946), p. 297.

37. Michael Reynolds, *The Young Hemingway* (Oxford: Basil Blackwell, 1986), p. 28.

38. Ibid., p. 24.

39. See Alice Hall Petry, *Fitzgerald's Craft of Short Fiction* (Tuscaloosa: The University of Alabama Press, 1989), p. 32.

40. See Matthew J. Bruccoli, *Some Sort of Epic Grandeur* (New York: Harcourt Brace Jovanovich, 1981), pp. 26–27 for Fitzgerald at age 12: "He played football as back or end—the inglorious line was not for him—on school and neighborhood teams, and was usually 'scared silly.' It was a matter of pride for him when he cracked a rib playing football. Scott's heroes at this time included Yale football star Ted Coy, Richard Harding Davis 'in default of someone better,' and Theodore Roosevelt."

41. This citation from Edwin Lawrence Godkin's *Unforeseen Tendencies of Democracy* (Boston and New York: Houghton Mifflin, 1898), pp. 225, 213 is from a book I have relied on for the reception of Reform and the literature it generated, John Fraser's *America and the Patterns of Chivalry* (Cambridge: Cambridge University Press, 1982), pp. 112–13.

42. Mencken, *A Mencken Chrestomathy,* pp. 229–42.

43. This citation from Roosevelt's *The Strenuous Life* (New York: Century Company, 1904), p. 282 is from Reynolds, p. 29.

44. Fraser has assembled some responses (pp. 121–22) to Roosevelt's youth-orientation:

> "If Roosevelt appealed to the public as strongly as he did, it was partly because of his persisting youthfulness. As Wells noted, 'in his undisciplined hastiness, his limitations, his prejudices, his unfairness, his frequent errors, just as much as in his force, his sustained courage, his integrity, his open intelligence, he stands for his people and his kind.' When he was police commissioner, a contemporary remarked that 'the peculiarity about him is that he has what is essentially a boy's mind.' And William Allen White recalled 'the infantile, or perhaps adolescent hunger in his heart' for danger that 'rendered him inexplicable [in the White House] to men of solemn and somber maturity.' Naturally, his career and personality were peculiarly attractive to the young."

Citations are, in order, from H. G. Wells, *The Future in America: A Search After Realities* (London: Chapman and Hall, 1906), p. 343; Joseph Bucklin Bishop, quoted by Henry F. Pringle in *Theodore Roosevelt: A Biography* (New York: Harcourt, Brace, 1931), p. 137; White, *Autobiography,* p. 348.

45. Lewis, *Main Street,* p. 11. The idea of "improvement" suffered the same fate as those other honorifics cited by Hemingway in *A Farewell to Arms.* Lewis comes to terms with change by showing the extent to which Carol's ideas have become dated. He makes sure that the dim-witted Raymie Wutherspoon condemns Balzac in favor of some "really improving story" that leaves out those disgusting "details" of actual personal life. In fact, Raymie prefers movies to books because (the time is approximately 1912) the former have been "thoroughly safeguarded by intelligent censors." There is a maniacally funny dialogue early in *Main Street* in which Carol finds out that Mrs. Luke Dawson thinks an "improving" book is almost as good as a sermon—but definitely not Swinburne. Carol tries to shove the ladies of the Thanatopsis club into the twentieth century, but they prefer to read *Culture Hints* about Men and Women of the Bible and Furnishings and China.

46. Theodore Roosevelt, *Theodore Roosevelt: An Autobiography* (New York: Da Capo, 1913), p. 17.

47. Ibid., pp. 346–49; 361.

48. William Dean Howells, *A Boy's Town* (New York: Harper & Brothers, 1890), p. 1.

49. Ibid., p. 175.

50. Bruccoli, ed., *The Short Stories of F. Scott Fitzgerald,* p. 33.

51. Cowley, ed., *The Stories of F. Scott Fitzgerald,* p. 309.

52. Bruccoli, ed., *The Short Stories of F. Scott Fitzgerald,* p. 413.

53. Booth Tarkington, "Richard Harding Davis," in *Van Bibber And Others* (New York: Charles Scribner's Sons, 1916), ix-xi.

54. Fitzgerald, *The Crack-Up,* p. 19.

55. Girouard, *The Return to Camelot,* p. 254. The lines on the spirit of chivalry cited from William Byron Forbush, *The Boy Problem* (6th edition, 1907), pp. 100–104.

56. Howells, *A Boy's Town,* pp. 68–71.

57. Girouard, *The Return to Camelot,* p. 282.

Index

RONALD BERMAN is professor of literature
at the University of California, San Diego.